FOREWORD

This book is dedicated to those who have been with me from the very beginning. Through the slow and fast miles, the easy and hard trails, I have relied on you as my unwavering support. At times, I have taken you for granted and not shown appropriate affection toward you, but I know that none of this would be possible without you. I will always love you and be grateful for your willingness to carry me through this journey. I love you, my dearest feet. Always and forever I will cherish you.

ACKNOWLEDGEMENTS

With a heart full of gratitude, I am humbled to think of all the people who have shown support for me not only in writing this book, but all along the winding path I started on decades ago that led me here. This book is a collection of essays about the experiences that have accumulated and slowly shaped who I am. I wrote this for the people who aren't afraid of chasing their dreams or inspiring others to do the same.

Austin, Olivia, Owen, and Evan, everything I do is to improve my role as your mother. It is my hope that as you have watched me set goals, work hard, learn, and grow that you have also been inspired to seek your passion in life. Each of you is intelligent, unique, and wonderful, with so much to contribute. Being your mother has been the most enjoyable adventure of my life and words can't express the depth of love I have for each of you. Believe in yourself and never stop thirsting for adventure.

For my Grandma. Through your example, I learned how to be a strong, independent woman. You inspired me with your adventurous soul and your ruthless work ethic. Mom and Dad, thank you for instilling self-confidence and a farm-girl-tough work ethic in me. I can't think of any two better characteristics to prepare a child to take on the world. To my husband, Rich: thank you for not trying to tame my wild heart.

And for my readers: may you be inspired to try something exciting and set a new goal. The richness it will bring to your life is beautiful. May none of us ever stop dreaming.

BIOGRAPHY

Tami Christensen lives in Gig Harbor, Washington. Tami was educated as an accountant, but after a decade working as a CPA in corporate America, she now finds joy in caring for her four children. While running marathons is her passion, she considers motherhood the best cross-training program. Nothing heals the body like housework and nothing heals the heart like sticky kisses, warm snuggles, and tight hugs from her kids. Tami is dreaming bigger and working harder for the next big goal. After all, the journey has just begun...

TO A GIRL I USED TO KNOW:

You're scared. I can see it in your eyes. Your fear is so palpable I feel compelled to reach out and grab it. Fear of the unknown can be paralyzing, so paralyzing that you might talk yourself out of having the courage to start this new adventure. You will be pushed out of your comfort zone into vulnerability, with failure not only a realistic outcome, but a certainty.

The truth is, you will fall flat on your face. You will feel failure so many times that failure won't scare you anymore. The sting of failure will lose its power over you. As you scrape yourself off the ground, you will learn about persistence, dedication, determination, and courage. Your body will cry in pain as you gather the mental strength to get up and keep going. Running will slowly strip away the layers of doubt, insecurity, and fear that the responsibilities of adulthood have placed upon you, until you are free to discover who you really are and who you were always meant to be. You will discover that you have the inner strength, perseverance, and courage you need to successfully navigate the challenges you face. As you push boundaries both internal and external, you will question why you accepted these boundaries in the first place.

What you don't know is that after you have failed, you will relish your small victories, knowing how hard you worked to earn those successes. You will gain far more than you lose. Having the courage to try again will give you grit. You will need the grit and persistence you learned through running to tackle life's constant challenges. You'll need them to work a full-time job while getting a master's degree, to move across the country several times, and to raise four children. In life as in running, you will be able to work through difficulties with preparation and determination. You will find that you can conquer anything you put your mind to if you are willing to work hard. When life knocks you down, your experiences as a runner will tell you to get up, dust yourself off, and keep trying until you cross that finish line.

Fear. Hope. Doubt. Excitement. Ignorance. Self-consciousness. Curiosity. Giddiness. Trepidation. Our emotions can feel raw, intimidating. Sign up for that marathon anyway. Commit to that goal, work hard, do your best, and trust yourself. You are wrapped in the cocoon of security and comfort. Training for a marathon will transform you and give you beautiful wings. Most importantly, it will forever alter your perspective. You weren't born to fail; you were born to fly! I believe in you.

Love,

The girl you are about to discover

LIFE ON THE RUN

*Only those who will risk going too far can possibly
find out how far one can go.*

—*T.S. Eliot*

Life is a beautiful journey of self-discovery and growth. Life's adventures lead to undiscovered and unexpected places. This is my story of running a 42K in each of the 50 states. As I've slipped on my shoes and let my mind ponder as my feet wander, I've found somebody I didn't know I was looking for. I found myself discovering thoughts and feelings hidden deep inside my soul. Like a fuzzy caterpillar emerging from a dark and warm cocoon, I've slowly emerged to find a changed person. The girl I found had learned that she could fly, and that changed everything. That girl was me, the real me who was hidden deep inside my body, waiting to be discovered. I stopped being a spectator of my own life and became an active participant, and it changed everything. As Thomas Carlyle once stated, "I've got a great ambition to die of exhaustion rather than boredom." My journey is one of ambition, discovered one mile at a time. All great adventures have a great story. In running 51marathons across the United States and DC, each training cycle has represented a piece of my life. When broken down into segments, each marathon represents decisions I have slowly worked through as I ran. When I string together the marathons I have completed, I see my life.

If you are looking for a technical running book complete with running plans, nutrition advice, training tips, and gear guides, what you find here will leave you disappointed. There are elite runners, coaches, and other experts who provide a plethora of information if you're looking for those details. This is the story of an ordinary girl who set an extraordinary goal. I am a weekend warrior, one who squeezes personal interests in between the duties of being a mother and wife, serving in my community, and maintaining a household. I did, however, decide to spend my free time going on a journey of self-discovery that led me to find who I truly was and what I wanted out of life. My hours on the run have given me quality time to reflect, to learn, and to make decisions, leaving me with a calculated clarity. This book is a collection of experiences and life lessons from my journey.

Running is my best—and sometimes my only—opportunity to think for extended periods of time, uninterrupted, exploring ideas, looking for learning opportunities.

I never quite know what an experience will teach me or what adventure next awaits, but running is the tool that calms my mind and body. I believe we all need something like that. We are all extraordinary, possessing unique skills and talents that make us amazing, and each of us has the ability to do something great. Discovering our hidden talents is part of the adventure and once we find the activity or practice that lets us connect with our inner self, we have the key to unlocking our potential.

Self-discovery is necessary for introspection and growth. Once the days of carefree childhood are over, as we become adults, we get to decide who we are and who we want to be. My story started in a small farming community in southern Idaho. If we had a lot of births and few deaths in any given year, we could maybe cheat our way up to a population of 1,200. My father was a farmer and cattleman out in the isolated desert we called home. It was a traditional 1950s-esque childhood setting. My father worked while my mother stayed home to care for me, my two sisters, and my brother. Living in the middle of nowhere gave my family hours on end to explore the great outdoors.

Since this is a book about running, you might assume that I grew up with a love of running. Nothing could be further than the truth. I loved dancing—rocky mountain clogging, to be specific. When I wasn't dancing, I loved to waterski on the Snake River, which flowed through my small, dozy town. Some of my fondest memories of growing up are rolling out of bed and grabbing a Diet Coke as we dashed off to the truck and drove down to the river.

If you were quick enough, you might get to sit inside the truck, where it was warm and void of insects. Otherwise, we rode in the back of the pickup, without seatbelts—this was long before seatbelts were recognized as valuable to human life—speeding down bumpy dirt roads.

In the back of the pickup, you learned quickly to keep your mouth shut so bugs didn't fly in. You also learned to sit low in case you hit a soft edge of the road or, even worse, the washboard bumps of the country roads.

Once my family got to the dock, we would unload the boat into the water and scramble to put on the wet suits. We only had three options: small, large, and too-bad-you-were-too-slow-so-you-get-nothing. If you happened to get stuck with the third option, you got to waterski in the chilly water. Being second in line for a used wet suit wasn't much better. The dash for wet suits was one of my first experiences with speedwork. Dad would drive the boat out to the middle of the river, lean backward and bellow, "Who is getting in? Someone get in or I'm throwing someone in." For the most part, I opted to do everything on my own accord. Plus, if you got thrown in, your face and hair went underwater. If I volunteered, I could ease into the water at my own speed.

At the age of eight, I learned how to water ski and shortly after I figured out how to slalom on one ski. I loved it. The rush and thrill of skiing on the water's smooth reflection made me fall in love with nature. Watching the sun come up over the mountains, ushering in a new morning, made me so grateful for this beautiful earth. Water skiing was where I learned to love both waking up with the sun and the endorphin high of an active body – two ingredients needed for the morning runner I have since become.

Running didn't enter my life until years later. I didn't run track or cross-country in junior high or high school. I began running as an adult. In an effort to fight family genetics and curb the side effects of my profession, which required me to sit at a desk working on a computer all day, a love affair with early morning workouts began. As I slipped out of the sheets and slipped my clothes on, I lost a little bit of sleep. But I gained more than I ever thought possible. In some ways I had lost myself in the blurry haze of growing from a child to an adult. The world sent what seemed like never-ending messages about who I should be, what I should do, and how to do it most efficiently. In the age of information, I had become a sponge and taken in what other people thought. And before long, I realized that I had buried myself under all those facts and opinions. Running helped me rediscover a new me, a better me. As I ran through experiences as a young adult, still figuring out life, I found a different person inside of me. She had been there all along. Mile after mile, I got to know her a little bit better. I grew to respect her, trust her, and like her. I came to realize that I didn't need to rely on external sources of information. I needed to rely on myself and my own thoughts as I faced my own dilemmas. As I ran, I realized that my own opinions and decisions were trustworthy. And I became happier with who I was and with my own choices.

When I began, I lacked any proper training on running or cross-training methods, and I felt like a bit of an imposter in the running community. But what I lacked in knowledge I made up for in passion. I loved the way running made my muscles burn and my heart beat. I loved how it made me sweat and exhausted my whole body. Over time, I grew to crave these feelings. And eventually, running became as natural and necessary to me as drinking water.

I signed up for my first marathon in September of 2003, and I quickly became hooked on the beautiful process of training, working hard, and finishing a race. After several marathons, I embarked on my goal to run a marathon in all 50 states, later to include D.C. to make it 51. In the years since that first race, I have moved nine times, changed jobs three times, and had four children. I started as a nervous beginner, unsure of being able to complete marathons to winning the women's divisions of marathons. Running transformed me as an athlete, but more importantly, it fundamentally transformed me as a person.

As I immersed myself in this goal, I found that there was a great deal I lost. I lost sleep. I lost my pride. I lost my ego. I lost fear. I lost my constant need to be in control of everything in my life. I lost a lot of myself. But, I gained so much more. I gained characteristics that have helped me live a life with more awareness. I learned how to persevere. I learned how to be flexible when life doesn't go as planned. I learned how to pick myself up after a disappointment and forge ahead. I learned how to forgive myself. I learned how to be as kind and understanding with my own shortcomings as I am with those of others. I learned how to set a goal and work hard. I learned to have courage. When it is all said and done, this book isn't about the miles I've run or how many marathons I've completed. It's about what lessons I learned out there on the road. These lessons are my life on the run.

PACK YOUR SUITCASE

"Be yourself. Everyone else is taken."

—*Oscar Wilde*

I love to travel. Having a fair view of the personality traits of my ancestors, if I had to identify the carrier of this expensive and never-satisfied travel gene, I would point my finger at my Grandma Patterson. She was a well-traveled woman and the most adventurous soul I've known. When I was growing up, her eyes sparkled as she told me about juicy peaches she'd eaten in the South and the fresh salmon from Alaska, the grandeur of Mount Rushmore, and the bright lights of New York City. She also collected small treasures from her foreign travel and displayed them in her home. Her extensive stories about her domestic and international travel sparked my curiosity to see this great big beautiful world. As I listened to her stories and looked at her treasures, I knew I wanted to see what she had seen. The sparkle in her eyes and the excitement in her voice as she told of her travels made her the most interesting woman I knew. When I was five, she gave me my first suitcase for Christmas.

Meize, as we have always called her, wisely advised packing a wallet full of clothes and a suitcase full of money, a practice at which she was an expert. She craftily devised a system where she would wear her shirt the proper way on day one and turn it inside out the second day, always sticking to solids so prints wouldn't betray her plan. If desperate, she would turn her shirt backward to squeeze out another day of wear. When traveling you rarely bump into the same people each day, so the likelihood of being identified as a clothing tightwad was slim to none. Well before the era of selfie sticks and social media, no one knew of her packing strategies except those of us who traveled with her. Either way, Meize couldn't care less. She was a wonderfully entertaining lady and people were drawn to her dazzling personality. No one cared what she wore.

Meize was a voluptuous woman with a perfectly soft grandmother's figure. A fox in her younger years, the life of a homemaker wore her out until she was immobilized by knee replacements. Family and friends, who were always welcome in her home, got spoiled with treats at her house, and she was an amazing cook. Cooking was how she showed her love. We had Norman Rockwell-style picturesque family dinners with mounds of food piled on the tables. Meize specialized in anything bread-related— loaves, rolls, cinnamon rolls, and desserts. There was also homemade peanut brittle, pies, caramels, ice cream, and everything else wonderfully and deliciously fattening. We lived a wonderful life of abundance and not once were we urged to temper our passions. If we wanted to eat an entire pie, Meize was happy to hand over a spoon while asking if she could get us a glass of milk to wash it down. As a natural result, we were a hefty bunch.

When I was a young kid, I happened to be using Meize's master bathroom when she was preparing for an upcoming trip. It was there that I saw her bra. She had a few personal items laid out as she prepared and packed for her upcoming trip. I didn't know how to properly snoop at this young age, so I am unable to report the cup size of this monstrosity, but I do recall being horrified. This bra, as hefty as it was, required four clasps on the back to be properly fastened, double the amount on the bra my mother wore. But the size of the bra was only the second-most shocking revelation. The biggest shock was what was inside it. Pinned into each bra cup were stacks of hundred dollar bills.

Fighting off my urge to leave the room before being caught, I couldn't resist finding out exactly how much cash she had stashed away. I counted into the thousands. I audited myself, unable to believe what my tiny little green eyes had just seen. Meize traveled with thousands of dollars! This confirmed two surprising facts. First, this little old lady—who to save money brought her own Sprite into McDonald's and bought dented cans at the grocery store—was not poor. She was LOADED. Second, she knew how to travel. Who needs a suitcase full of money when you have a bra that size.

Unfortunately, my bra size only allows me to hide a few bills in each cup before giving off the puckered and lumpy look. And, sadly, I am a bit more proud than Meize. I remember being mortified, the times we traveled together, when the dinner tab would come and she would reach down the front of her shirt, unpin the safety pin, and fish out a few sweaty bills. As she handed them over, the waitress's perplexed look summarized my feelings: gross! Meize was always generous, and it wasn't unusual for her to slip a moist, sticky bill into my hand when I found the perfect souvenir. This always left me feeling uneasy. I had to choose between holding a sweaty boob bill or rejecting the cold hard cash. Always, I overcame my germaphobic nature long enough to slip the bill into my pocket.

When I think about Meize's house, I recall a home full of memories. Her home wasn't cluttered. Meize and Gramps weren't materialistic at all. She wore the same clothes for decades, and only had a few outfits to begin with. Gramps had very basic needs as well. They didn't value quality or quantity of material possessions. To them, aside from the people they collected in their lives, knowledge and experience were the most valuable possessions of all. In Meize's guest bathroom, she had a beautiful vase filled with layers of sand she had collected from all over the world. The sand was all different colors, each beautiful and glorious in its own right. She told me that it reminded her that just like the sand, the countries she had visited and the people she met were equally diverse and wonderful.

Traveling was an indulgence and an opportunity for an education. As she told me of her grand adventures, I was mesmerized. She was the most interesting person I had ever met. She seemed so well rounded and wise. She was not only my loving Meize, she was someone I wanted to be just like. Through her traveling experience, Meize had learned how to communicate and touch people. While there may have been differences between ethnicities, cultures, and geography, she was able to make a friend out of anyone and connect with others by focusing on their similarities rather than their differences.

Meize made friends everywhere she went. She got stranded in an airport after a sudden snowstorm, and received an invitation to stay at a pilot's home for the evening. She routinely had visitors from out of town who were friends she made while traveling. Once you became her friend, you were her friend forever. Her life was full, beautiful, and rich because of the experiences she had and the people she surrounded herself with. She showed me that experiences and people could touch and change my life in a much more profound way than any material item I could purchase.

Traveling has been a source of joy at every phase of my life. My childhood was marked with family vacations in and out of the country. Meize and Gramps always joined in for the fun, which only added to the enjoyment. Over the years, my family traveled several times to Hawaii, a couple of times to Mexico, and took plenty of road trips. The first trip I remember taking was a road trip to Yellowstone. Meize, always frugal, packed along a brick of cheddar cheese, several loaves of bread, and a tube of ham that she kept in a cooler between the front seats. Any time we were hungry on the drive to, from, or around Yellowstone, we were given three choices of sandwiches: cheese, ham or cheese and ham. Meize redeemed herself though, also packing goody boxes full of bread, candy, cookies, and popcorn balls. Always, we could find a stack of cash hidden inside her goody box.

While I've traveled across the states and have been outside the country exploring Mexico, South America, Asia and Europe, my appetite to explore the rest of the world remains unquenched. Meize made it to destinations I have yet to see. When I hear about the pyramids in Egypt, the Great Barrier Reef in Australia, or the view from Machu Picchu, and when I think of the stories she once shared with me, I feel a magnet in my body drawing me to those places. I want my life to be full of the types of adventures Meize had. I want to meet fascinating people, in the United States and around the world. I want to be interesting and well rounded like Meize.

As I pack my bags to travel around the country for my races I stick by a few of my grandmother's traveling philosophies. First, you will find something exciting to see or a fun spot to visit everywhere you travel. Some places there will be many choices and it will be hard to sift through all your options. Other times, you will have to really dig to find a hidden gem. Second, people are generally helpful and friendly as long as you are nice to them. Talk to everyone, because you can learn something from anyone. Meize and Gramps had the gift of the gab, making a friend out of anyone because of the respect they showed others and the interest they took in their lives. If you treat people with kindness and respect, most of the time they will do whatever they can to help you. Third, don't eat anything you aren't familiar with. Eating local food can be fun, but since this book is about my travels relating to running marathons, I'll take the stance that I'm grateful for Subway restaurants. I eat the same sandwich before and after my races. Lastly, very few travel mishaps are actually emergencies. A cancelled flight, a missed flight, a missing reservation, lost luggage—most issues that arise can easily be fixed with a smile, patience, and kindness.

Exploring the United States and the world is a valuable treasure I'll never take for granted. I've climbed the watch towers of the Great Wall of China and as I was climbing on top of this historic landmark, I looked over to Mongolia to see the most stunning mountain range. While exploring Paris, I hiked to the top of the Eiffel tower to see the iconic city. In Prague (my most favorite city of all time), I wandered from the Old Town to the New Town along the Vltava river. In London, we hopped from the London Tower to the London Bridge sliding onto the London Eye. In Barcelona I walked up and down Las Rambalas, enjoying the street festivities and shops. And Germany, I was grateful for not only my physical health, but my freedoms as I walked through a concentration camp. I squeezed through the narrow spiral stairs of the Blarney Castle only to hang upside down to kiss the famous Blarney stone. A sense of adventure and curiosity is one of the greatest gifts my parents, Gramps, and especially Meize gave me—which is why I got my kids all got little suitcases for Christmas.

CHASING DREAMS

"You are never too old to set another goal or to dream a new dream."

—*C.S. Lewis*

On winding dirt country roads, I learned how to drive when I was six years old. I drove ATVs and motorcycles at a younger age, but most of all I loved driving my dad's truck. I had to sit on the edge of the front seat to reach the gas and brake pedals while peering over my knuckles at the steering wheel, sitting tall with a straight back so I could see the road and touch the pedals at the same time. I loved the purr of the diesel engine. Dad knew how much I loved driving his truck and when I was finishing eighth grade he made a deal with me. If I got straight As in high school, graduated valedictorian, and went to a good college on a scholarship, he would use the money the scholarship would save to let me buy any truck I wanted. He knew this was the one thing that would motivate my thirteen-year-old self as I entered the ninth grade to get the best grades possible.

Dad wasn't letting me off the hook easy. He knew I could take easy classes and maintain a 4.0. But in order to achieve his objective of getting into a good college with a scholarship, I'd need to take challenging electives and classes like calculus, advanced chemistry, biology, and accounting. While the lifetime sports class was appealing to me, Dad wouldn't allow it—he referred to easy classes as "underwater basket weaving," a total waste of time. The advanced placement classes would be hard, but he had a lot of confidence in me. Moreover, he firmly believed that high school should prepare me for college, not retirement. And, as he often reminded me, if I tried to do something amazing and fell a little short, I was still better off than if I tried to do something average.

As with any long-term goal, at first it was easy to stay focused and motivated, but as time went on and the demands for my time and attention increased, it became more difficult. I had to learn how to manage my time very well and multitask in order to accomplish what I needed to do and what I wanted to do. I slept less and had less down time. But the skills I acquired have lasted me far beyond the high school years. I became efficient. I learned how to be dedicated. I saw that big goals are achievable, but they often happen though small persistent steps along the way. When aggregated, those tiny forward movements will eventually get you to the goal.

I sat in the front row during high school graduation with the rest of those graduating at the top of the class with high honors. Conflicting emotions filled my body as I turned to look at my family in the stands. They had helped me set a high goal for myself. They had encouraged me along the way. I looked at my fellow classmates, many of whom I had taken classes with. We had done it. I had done it. I had sacrificed and worked hard to have the honor of graduating valedictorian. I had learned to set long-term goals and to steadily work toward them. I liked this feeling of satisfaction, and I decided right then and there that I would continuously set goals for myself to make sure I kept growing as an individual. I felt a wave of gratification spread over my body as I enjoyed the fruits of my labor. The feeling was so strong it was almost palpable. I knew I would chase that sense of accomplishment again.

The catalyst for setting this goal had been feeling the power of a diesel engine as I gripped the steering wheel, but I negotiated a much better reward upon graduation. I chose to attend a private college that was more expensive (and used my truck money for tuition not covered by scholarships and living expenses)—plus I was also able to attend the Hawaii extension campus. This meant no truck, but this was a tradeoff I was happy to make!

Opportunities continued to present themselves and I continued to set goals. Thanks to taking full loads of credits, attending college year-round, and picking my major early on, I graduated from college in fewer than the typical four years. I studied for the GMAT, the Graduate Management Admission Test, and gained admission to a master's program while working as an accountant in a corporate office. My life thus far had been a series of cause and effect where I would set a goal, work hard, and achieve it. As my confidence grew, my boldness in setting goals also grew. I felt independent, confident, strong, and capable. The self-satisfaction that came from doing something hard was amazing. I had become addicted to the feeling.

Most of the goals I set for myself have been impromptu in nature, something that strikes me that falls within my interests. I will find a passion and decide to invest time and energy into it. When I decided to run a marathon in all 50 states, I had already been running marathons and knew I enjoyed traveling—those were two of my biggest passions. When I heard there were people who set out to run marathons in every state, I latched onto that as my goal immediately.

While I loved my profession, work was still work. After I became a parent I eventually transitioned to primarily staying home with my kids. As much as I enjoyed motherhood and the comradery I found with other mothers, I refused to hang my self-esteem on my children. Always fiercely independent, I wanted to be an individual. I wanted to do something spectacular on my own. Running marathons is something I personally enjoy and get great satisfaction out of, but since becoming a mother, my desire to run marathons is now twofold: running for myself and running for my children. I want my children to be inspired to set goals and work hard. I want them to dream big, the way my dad taught me to. As I thought about how my children would see me, my motivation increased. Would they see me simply as the woman who did their dishes, not knowing all that I was capable of? Would I be remembered as the household cook, maid, nurse, and chauffeur? Would I have the opportunity to show them I was much more than that?

I wanted to be the mom who took them to the lake to swim, baked their favorite cookies, and threw fun parties. I also wanted to be an inspiration to them. As my children grew, I wanted them to see that setting goals, big and small, is a lifelong process. Education doesn't stop after high school and college. Striving for excellence is a way of life, without an expiration date. I wanted them to remember my words encouraging them to dream big and work hard. But, I also wanted them to see me do that myself.

I wanted my children to see that failure is part of trying and struggling toward a goal is part of life. I don't achieve every goal I set the first time. My kids see me go out and run in freezing temps or when it is raining heavily outside. They notice when I limp around the house after a grueling long run. When I head out the door for yoga instead of watching TV, they know I am doing it for my overall health. My children have had a front-row seat to how important it is to take care of yourself physically, emotionally, and mentally.

After each marathon, I come home and tell my family about my experience. Some tales relay victory and self-satisfaction. Other races are hard and the results aren't what I was hoping for. Every morning they see how I have incorporated running into my life. They know I have to work hard and be persistent in inching my way toward my objective. We are all capable of doing big things. What differentiates those who succeed from those who fail is dedication. I wanted them to see me succeeding and realizing my dreams. I want them to know that they can realize their dreams. Above all, I wanted them to know that they were the reason I was inspired to be a better person. Knowing that I had four children who were watching me, observing my behaviors, and learning from how I lived my life made me a better person, runner, and mother.

Teaching moments with my children are, like my goals, mostly impromptu in nature. We may be sitting at a stoplight on the way to school when my son will tell me about a challenge he is facing. Using my experience in marathon running, I can relate to him, empathize with his feelings, and share advice. When my children ask why I choose to eat healthy, I am able to educate them to make healthier choices for themselves. Knowing that discouragement is the roadblock to progress, I can share with them my most painful failures and the process I went through to overcome it. Being able to look them in their shiny little hopeful eyes and have relatable conversations is what helps reduce the roadblocks they face down to temporary stumbling blocks.

Running a marathon in all 50 states would take years of daily dedication. I would need to train year-round. I knew that planning marathon weekends would require some massaging of the family schedule and at times would be costly. As life has ebbed and flowed, I've run marathons when I could. Some years, I was able to race more. Other years, I had a new baby and had to take time off during pregnancy. Just as when I'd set the goal to graduate valedictorian, I didn't recognize all of the difficulties that would arise beforehand. I didn't realize how demanding and difficult it would be at times to maintain the persistence necessary to succeed.

Marathon running changed for me as I got older and it has certainly become more difficult to juggle and multitask. Our weekends used to be so calm when the children were babies, and now they are the busiest part of the week, filled with seasonal sports like soccer games and snow skiing. Birthday parties, church, and gatherings with friends fill what little down time we have. My body recovered a lot more quickly when I was younger; as I've aged, I feel more stiff and sore. Yes, running has taken its toll on me. At times I've wondered if I should abandon my goal or put it on pause. It was hard to keep focused on completing a goal over so many successive years of being a mother to little children. But I had learned through previous experience that every noteworthy goal is difficult to reach. And so I forged ahead.

Fourteen years and five weeks after I ran my first marathon, I will complete my goal. I will have more children than I did when I started. Those four sweet little children will have somehow grown from babies to young people during that time. Initially, I started racing as a young professional when I could pack a bag, throw it in the car, and drive to my marathons over the weekend. Then, I became a mother and I prepared for my weekends away by making sure laundry was done, bottles were mixed, baby food was blended, and diapers and wipes were stocked up. Now I am masterful at scheduling soccer games, carpools, dance recitals, and birthday parties, on top of the food and clothing preparation while maneuvering a marathon weekend.

As I look back at the last 14 years, I feel that same warm feeling inside that I did when I sat in the front row of my high school graduation. My confidence has grown as I have learned and become a better person. This experience has changed me in more ways than I thought possible. I did something hard and I didn't quit when I ran into obstacles. I had to dig deeper than I thought I could. I persevered and stayed focused even when it got really hard. I have inspired my children to do hard things. They know what hard work looks like. Like Dad said, it's good to try to do something amazing. Sometimes you fall short, but other times you exceed your own expectations.

DRIVE

"To give anything less than the best is to sacrifice the gift."

—*Steve Prefontaine*

I look at the beautiful brand-new baby in my arms, grateful for such a wonderful little gift. I am lucky to be entrusted with this miracle. I lean forward and whisper into the baby's tiny ear a promise I intend on keeping until the day I leave this earth. I promise to love the baby and take care of it the best I know how. I've made this promise to each one of my four babies as they lay in my arms.

As I whisper these words, I feel a wave of inadequacy. I don't know what my best is. I want to be someone my baby will look up to as an inspiration. I want to be someone who teaches through action what so many words can't say. I want them to be happy and I know that a big part of happiness is feeling accomplished. Self-esteem often derives from success. What does success look like for me? How am I going to show these babies what it means to find passion in life? To be unafraid to try new things? To push beyond self-doubt into a territory where they feel freedom?

Striving to be the best mom possible is a life-long commitment. I know that at times I will fail miserably, but it won't be for lack of effort. My intentions and desires are pure. I also know that to be the best mom to my babies, I need to be happy and fulfilled myself. And that is why I run.

As I hold my baby, I look out the window and find myself daydreaming about running, imagining the feel of the wind in my hair, of sweat dripping down my back. Breathing hard, pushing myself faster, feeling empowered. More than anything, I just want to go for a run, free, for the first time since pregnancy began, from the weight of a baby pressing on my joints. As much as I love this moment, here in the hospital with my beloved newborn, part of me still wishes I were on a trail with the sun on my skin. The hospital requires that I stay for at least 24 hours, but as soon as I get home I will slip on my shoes and begin the process of returning to myself.

Running is ingrained in me. No matter what else is happening, it's a part of my life. I have only taken a handful of days off in the last two decades. With each of my kids I ran every day of pregnancy up until the day they were born, luckily able to continue activity without too much discomfort. Though my pace slowed, I relished this part of my life, grateful that I could continue to run even as I manufactured a human being.

When people ask what motivates me to get up in the morning and run, I don't quite know how to respond. It's like asking if I want to get up and breathe. I can't imagine a daily routine that doesn't include sweat, endorphins, and fresh air. It's something I enjoy, crave, desire, NEED. It makes me a better person, mother, daughter, wife, and friend. And more than anything it makes me happy.

Running every day isn't a matter of if, but more of a question of what type of run my body needs. On a bright, sunny day when I feel energized and alert, I do speedwork. When I feel tired and have low energy, I take a recovery day. My workout syncs up with my mood so running feels therapeutic, not like a chore. Long runs are always good for working through the heavy thinking backlog. There is a run for every day and every mood.

I love what running shows me, the time it gives me to think and to observe. What will I learn from today's run about the world outside my body or about myself? What will I see? What will inspire me? Will today be the day that I work through a problem that has been nagging my mind for weeks?

I love the way running pushes me. I'm curious how much faster and stronger I can get, how far I can go, how much more I can demand of my body. I won't know unless I keep going until I find my limits. There is something inside me that continues to plant seeds of curiosity in my mind, questions about my current limitations and boundaries. Accomplishment isn't noteworthy in itself; it is striving to be your best that counts. We each have our own version of our best effort, and I know when I've put forth mine. Wondering if I have given my very best inspires me to keep pushing harder, to prove to myself that I am.

There is a theory known as the "10,000 Hour Rule" based on a study from K. Anders Ericsson, a Swedish psychologist. He asserted that when a person has been engaged in a specific activity for 10,000 hours, that person becomes an expert in that talent or skill. Malcolm Gladwell, a social economist, illustrated this point in his book Outliers, in which he focuses on numerous individuals who have met success once they've passed the threshold of 10,000 hours. As I approach this magical number with running, I see the benefits of my dedication. My body is becoming more efficient. My times are getting faster. Recovery is easier. Running is easier. I know that until I can't go any farther or faster, I have not yet reached my potential. I have an internal drive to meet my limit. It feels like a hurricane with full-force winds, unstoppable, blowing through anything in its path.

Running gives me more than piece of mind, more than fitness, more than time outside. Running has led me to set goals, to try to tackle the impossible, to see what happens when I come out the other side. To an outsider, the goal of running a marathon in all 50 states might not make a lot of sense. It comes with no financial gain or reward. But for me, striving for excellence is reward enough. More than anything I value the non-monetary reward of being able to look into my kids' eyes and tell them to work hard because it's worth it. The satisfaction from working hard is enough in itself. I want them to see me trying to become better, to see me do things I'm proud of. I want to be an example to them, someone who will inspire them to keep striving for their own passions. Self-satisfaction is worth more than a mountain of gold.

Running a marathon in all 50 states once seemed like an insurmountable goal—and yet here I am, goal almost achieved, now aware that I am capable of even more. What? I don't know. Perhaps the curiosity of finding out is the very process I enjoy. With a restless heart, I wonder how I can take running to the next level

I suppose there are two types of people, the "whys" and the "why nots." I fall into the latter category. Why not push to find my limits? Why not try to get better? What do I have to lose? This approach has led to some of the best adventures in my life. If there is anything I want my children to remember and emulate about me, it's that they should always try to be the best version of themselves they possibly can. And unlike that promise I whispered in their tiny newborn ears, I keep this promise daily in my heart. I promise that no matter what, their mother loved them more than herself. And because of that promise I made, I am determined to be my best.

ADDICTION

They say you can't run away from your troubles.
I say you can.

—*John Bingham*

I'll confess, I'm borderline OCD anxious and neurotic. I have a Type A personality and I can be high-strung. Once I delve into a project, it becomes all-consuming. I've always been this way. In the fourth grade I became obsessed with the book series The Baby-Sitters Club. I would stay in my room and read a whole book in a day. I relished every plot twist, every dramatic event, and every emotion as if I were one of the main characters. I can still recall my favorite characters and their personalities nearly thirty years later. As soon as I finished one book, I had to read the next. I needed closure and completion. It's who I am and how I am with every aspect of my life.

My OCD behavior is clearly demonstrated through my love for Diet Coke, which has long held its grasp on my soul. I had my first sip when I was at my best friend Emily's house. I didn't like the sweet taste of regular Coke so she gave me one of her dad's Diet Cokes. One swallow and I was hooked. I was too young to make any grocery list demands, and my parents didn't like the idea of my drinking soda pop or consuming caffeine, so at first it was a little secret treat I would get only when I went to Emily's house. But things soon escalated.

A perk of living in a small town is that everyone knows one another. Dad had a charge account at the two gas stations that were situated diagonally from each other at the one stoplight in town. We also had a charge account at the town's only grocery store. The gas stations and grocery store were "on your honor" businesses where you could eat the candy bar as you walked around, taking the chocolaty wrapper to the clerk on your way out. I had been accompanying my parents into these stores since I could walk, so they all knew who I was. They knew my dad was good for the bill and I was given permission to charge anything I wanted. At the end of each month, the gas stations and grocery store would send my parents a sum of the total charges. Without a detailed accounting of my purchases, my splurge I used to save for Emily's house became a more regular occurrence, one I indulged with every stop at the gas station. I had unlimited access to the secret sauce.

When I was in high school, I often used my lunch money to purchase Diet Coke instead of food. When my parents found out about this, they started giving me more money so I could buy both Diet Coke and food. Like a true addict, I just bought twice as much Diet Coke. I craved it and couldn't get enough. I loved the feeling of the carbonated drink sliding down my throat, the energy high I would get from the caffeine, and the full feeling after drinking a soda pop. School lunch was unappealing and I much preferred spending the lunch hour socializing with my friends to eating anyway. My parents believed all the soda pop was bad for my bones and tried to get me to quit. I just became really good at stashing Diet Coke in my room so I could crack open a can of that dark, delicious, bubbly sweet nectar of life whenever I wanted. These days, I have a fountain soda pop machine in my garage with Diet Coke on tap so I can grab a cold one at any point. Go big or go home!

I know addiction and I welcome it like an old friend. I like the indulgence of having something I enjoy. The truth is I think everyone who is good at something has a passion. That passion is often an obsession and an obsession can easily become an addiction. Addictions can ruin lives and the power addiction can have on someone can be devastating if that addiction is unhealthy. It is with respect to my addictive personality and the addictive powers that I recognize my weaknesses and draw boundaries around my addictions. I know, as little things like an obsession with Diet Coke (and my other obsession, M&M's) have taught me, that I have an addictive personality. And because of this, I also know that I have to be very careful about what I let myself delve into. Running is my good physical addiction, while Diet Coke and Peanut M&M's

are my indulgences, my vices. However, because they are not illegal or immoral, society doesn't judge me harshly for them.

A personal belief that I latched onto is "if it is worth doing, it is worth doing right." As a natural overachiever, I throw myself into everything I do with all my effort. Whether it is Peanut M&M's, Diet Coke, my academics, running, or parenting, I throw myself in the deep end. It's who I am, the fabric I was cut from. My family ingrained the idea of perseverance and dedication to a task or habit. Growing up on the farm, we knew we had to follow directions and do our best or there would be negative consequences. A job half done is a job not done at all. Given my natural proclivities, the best thing I know how to do is attempt to pick the healthiest and most productive (or least destructive) addictions to channel my addictive personality toward.

When a person is addicted to an activity such as work, society praises and rewards those people. They get promotions, they get recognition within the organization and from their peers, they get compensated better, and they get a collective pat on the back. Exercising can also fit into this category of "positive addiction." People will shower praise for putting a priority on health and fitness. People will gush with admiration for a feat accomplished, acknowledging how difficult it must have been. These are those secret pats on the back that athletes love to receive.

Wikipedia defines behavioral addiction as a compulsion to engage in a natural reward—which is a behavior that is inherently rewarding—despite adverse consequences.

Running multiple marathons within a year, year after year, decade after decade, definitely falls into this category. It is also one of those behavioral addictions society has deemed acceptable.

There is a fine line between a dedicated runner and someone who is obsessed. The euphoric high I get from running feels so good, it will alter my mood for hours and potentially days. It makes my life more enjoyable and happy, so I continue to search for that feeling as I slip my running shoes on each morning. Everyone needs an outlet for stress. But when does an activity cross the line from an enjoyable habit to a problem? And who gets to decide which activities are acceptable addictions to have? If a person is addicted to gambling, pornography, shopping, smoking, drugs, or alcohol, most would agree that those addictions can have negative side effects.

The endorphins that are released during exercise activate opiate receptors, giving off a euphoric feeling. The release of these opiate receptors causes the brain to have pain relief much like what drugs can provide. An exercise addict will feel a compulsion to repeat the activity until she gets that feeling again. Unfortunately the amount of exercise needed to achieve that release of endorphins increases over time and the exercise intensity also needs to increase.

When I first started running, I went a couple of times a week for 30 minutes. Over time, it became a personal challenge to see how far I could go and how fast I could run. Slowly but surely, I became an endorphin junkie. Anything extreme got me excited. I loved pushing my boundaries to see the improvement. In doing so, I became a textbook addict. So it begs the question: is it a bad thing to be an addict? As long as society gives a nod of approval to the addiction, and it's not directly or negatively harming anyone, is it okay?

As much happiness as my addictions bring me, I know they have impacted my life in positive and negative ways. I'm one of the lucky ones. My addictions, the way I cope with life, are healthy. I recognize how fortunate I am. When I wake before 5:00 a.m., getting up as the sun peeks over the mountains, I miss the opportunity to snuggle with my kids if they've crawled into bed. My self-imposed early bedtime (necessitated by those early mornings) means I miss the opportunity to stay up late with friends on the weekend. I've missed out on some things, but I've experienced many more. My addictions have brought pure joy into my life that outweighs the negative side effects.

PREPARATION

*"Make sure your worst enemy doesn't live between
your own two ears."*

—*Laird Hamilton*

Ah, the best-laid plans. It had taken more than a year to
plan our grand adventure: a cruise along the coast of the
beautiful state of Alaska, time away from home with a
backdrop of mountains, glaciers, and wildlife. On a cruise
along the coast of the beautiful state of Alaska, my family
was enjoying spending time away. I had been planning our
grand adventures for a year and our kids were so excited
to see and do the activities we had been talking about for
months. I had packed for our family of six. This, alone, is
deserving of an award. At the very least, a massage and a
large, ice-cold Diet Coke. But, alas. Despite my disappointment in the lack of kudos being thrown my way, we had

thrown our suitcases into the car and loaded up our children. The first leg of our journey was the six-hour drive to Vancouver, British Columbia. We had planned a mini-vacation before the cruise to enjoy some local activities before we embarked on the Disney Magic, which would sail along the western coast of the United States. I, in my meticulous planning, had packed our bags as if we were going on two vacations. That way, we wouldn't need to carry in and sort through all of our suitcases to access the items we would need for the few days in Vancouver. I had vacationing down to a science, a perfect, airtight process.

I had the diapers, wipes, jackets, changes of clothes, surprise gifts for the kids, shoes, socks, cruise documents, passports, and baby snacks, all of it snugly packed away. We left our driveway filled with excitement for the adventures that lay ahead. The drive from eastern Washington to Vancouver went perfectly, a small miracle given that we were traveling with our four small children, several of whom normally get carsick. Having somehow avoided traffic and not needing our usual multiple stops to help queasy passengers, the trip was starting out wonderfully. I sat in the passenger seat feeling gloriously satisfied as our vacation progressed without the slightest glitch. I basked in the glow of my success, so very proud of myself for planning and arranging an amazing family trip that would surely be immortalized in my children's memories forever. I was nothing but 100% pure awesomeness.

We arrived in Vancouver and enjoyed the adventures I'd planned there for the few days before the cruise would depart. My method of packing, with separate luggage for vacation stop #1, worked wonderfully; I would log its raging success in my long-term memory for future use. It was genius, and having been the author of such an idea, I was also a genius! By the time we had checked into our stateroom on the cruise, my self-satisfaction was at an all-time high. I had really outdone myself this time. And our first day on the cruise was even more magnificent than I could have planned. The kids danced their hearts out at the sailing party, and we quickly jumped into the ship's activities and fine dining.

We tucked in that night after a busy day of travel and drifted off to sleep with smiles on our faces. Every parent's dream is to give their kids fun, wholesome experiences to build wonderful childhood memories. We had hit a home run—and by "we," I certainly meant that I had hit a home run. In our household we divide and conquer the family tasks and it is my sole responsibility to plan and execute all family vacations, from coming up with itineraries to packing everyone's suitcases.

The next morning I snuck out for an early run before anyone got up, like I usually do. I came back and showered before waking up my husband, Rich. As we prepared ourselves for the day of activities, Rich asked me if I could remember where I put his underwear when I was unpacking. It was in one of the drawers, I assured him. Just look a little harder.

He looked hard. Then he looked a little harder. He still couldn't locate his drawers and because his questions were starting to annoy me, I finally agreed to see for myself. Convinced that he was only looking at the clothes at the top of each pile, I really dug into each drawer until I was forced to face the truth. I had forgotten to pack his underwear. And we were on a cruise that didn't sell men's underwear. Oops! I had researched, planned, prepared, and almost executed the perfect getaway, only to overlook a major—unmentionable—detail.

Despite our best efforts, small or large oversights in preparation can diminish the satisfaction of our experience. Preparing for races is no different. We pick a training plan and pour ourselves into following it down to every detail. It often feels as if the more strictly we adhere to the plan, the better our results will be. We meticulously monitor our diets, our sleep, the miles we log on our running shoes, our perfect race weight. We purchase airfare and book hotels based on which has the best distance to the race's start and finish. Every little detail is planned for optimal results.

In my less experienced days of training for marathons, I'd shift my weekend long runs to a different morning whenever the weather was less than ideal. Living in the Pacific Northwest, it is common to have rainstorms blow in unexpectedly, the wind howling. When snow dumps it often falls quickly and brutally. When this happened on my long run day, I'd reschedule for a different day of the weekend. I didn't need to train in terrible conditions; my race would likely have calm weather, I'd assure myself.

Several years ago, I flew out to Oklahoma City, Oklahoma, to run the Memorial Marathon in May. May is a popular month for marathons because the heavy part of the training is done in March and April when weather is usually mild, and race weather is generally ideal. But May in Oklahoma turned out to be wet. On race day, the rain was pouring and the clouds were so dark they were almost black. My running partner, Vicki, and I could hear the thunder cracking as busloads of runners were dropped off from the various surrounding hotels. We congregated in a stadium to stay dry, all of us desperately hoping the rain would let up.

Since it is a lot of work to schedule a race, train for a race, and organize a weekend away, I wanted to run. At the same time, I didn't want to run in the rain. I wasn't even sure the organizers would allow the race to continue because of the thunder and fears of lightening. The race directors delayed the start, hoping the rain would lighten, the thunder would stop, and the lightning wouldn't show up at all.

I was not equipped to handle these conditions, mentally or physically. I had planned well, but not for this. I had never trained in a downpour. I hadn't packed adequate clothing for several hours of running in the rain. I wasn't sure if I was mentally ready to tackle this marathon. I was unprepared.

As I sat there, it dawned on me: in all my meticulous preparation, I had planned for everything except the unexpected. I hadn't trained in pouring rain, whipping wind, or frigid blizzards. I'd hit the Easy button, snuggled up to the cozy fireplace, and waited for a more comfortable time to go for a long run. I had failed to properly prepare for the unexpected. I was physically strong and mentally weak!

I ran the marathon—every wet, soggy, and miserable inch of the course. I whined and complained each step of the way. My feet were blistered from wet socks rubbing against my skin. I had inflamed chafing under my arms, around my chest, and on my legs. The thunder rolled and the rain came down, but I forced myself to keep going. I had come this far and my plane didn't leave for a few more hours. I might as well fill my time with something productive like running a marathon, I told myself. Dig deep and soldier up!

Oftentimes, we miss the mark. One little detail is overlooked, or there is one variable we can't control that changes everything. We try to prepare our best for the adventure ahead, but the reality is that our plans won't be executed exactly as we'd envisioned. It happens, and it happens to all of us. The unexpected challenges are not the most important part of the experience. The most important part is what we decide to do next.

In the end, we enjoyed the cruise in Alaska and I successfully finished the Oklahoma marathon. Each of those experiences helped teach me to increase mental strength and make accommodations for the unexpected. I no longer give myself the luxury of moving my long training runs to days with better conditions. I force myself to run in the cold, wind, rain, snow, and early hours, knowing that by doing so, I am preparing myself for a marathon where I will meet Mother Nature in one of those forms. And while I can't prepare for every variable, increasing mental strength will help me face challenges with greater ease.

I was able to push through the discomfort of the bad weather in Oklahoma, and my husband kept his grumbling to a dull roar regarding his commando Alaskan vacation. I gave him the same wise words of advice I tell myself: dig deep and soldier up! A week of wearing no underwear is not something you can train or prepare for, but it's also not something that needs to ruin a trip.

I learned another great lesson through this experience: it is much easier to tell someone to soldier up than it is to do it yourself. Which leads me to one last tip. If you ever find yourself telling your husband to soldier up and go commando for a week, being able to run fast is certainly a necessity.

BLINDNESS

*"Those that know, do. Those that
understand, teach."*

—Aristotle

It wasn't the first time I had seen it. But although I'd seen it before, each time it surprised me. The shock, the confusion, the peace and love that followed, all these raw emotions seemed to strike a chord in my soul. The man running a marathon next to me was blind, holding a rope. The woman next to him held the other end, and she would guide him from the start to the finish as they ran the next 26.2 miles together.

The mind picks and chooses how it interprets its surroundings and internalizes them. It's funny how lessons in life are right in front of us. When you are finally ready to see what has been there all along, it somehow feels like a new experience. Whether it's the first snowfall of the winter season with the great big fluffy flakes that makes you stop and see how beautiful a winter wonderland can be, or perhaps the perfect breeze on a sunny day at the beach when you realize how the sun dances on the water as the waves perfectly crest. Sometimes it can be something as tiny as the dimple on your little boy's cheek when he smiles, perfectly framing his little lips, acting as a microphone for his belly laugh. The sight strikes you so profoundly and deeply, your breath is taken away like it's the first time witnessing the grandeur of the event. In these moments my spirit is so humble and thoughtful that I'm at my most teachable.

I saw the blind man as we crossed paths on the marathon course, a small paved path that ran parallel to the river that flows through Bismarck, North Dakota. He was an older gentleman with a wrinkled face. It was a beautiful, sunny fall day, and like most people, he appeared to be squinting from the brightness. But, on a closer look, he was different. His eyes were deeply sunken, and instead of squinting, they were completely shut. He was also running unusually close to his partner. A black rope stretched between them. He held onto one end and his partner held onto the other so she could guide him along the course. He stayed half a step to her diagonal. He knew when she went down the curb, around a pothole, when she turned right and when she turned left. She slowed her pace on the uphill climb and would lean back during the downhill parts of the course. He was so intimately familiar with her running form and movement that, feeling the tension of the rope, he knew how to adjust his body to prepare for the course ahead. When necessary, she would verbalize any warnings or advice that were also needed to keep him safe.

The first time I saw a blind runner was at the Chicago Marathon in October of 2011. Chicago is the second biggest marathon in the United States. The crowds of spectators and volunteers plus the tens of thousands of runners meant we were all congested along the downtown streets. For miles, we ran elbow to elbow with each other. Not long into the race, I noticed a woman who was constantly shouting out comments. It seemed that every half a minute, she was giving a man near her an update on the course. The man's eyes were sunken in, with a glossy white film that was barely exposed. He was blind. The woman runner was guiding this man through a mass of people in addition to navigating the course. Incredibly, her guiding words kept him safe from potential dangers, and acted as a sounding horn notifying other runners of the man's needs. I was amazed at the dedication and love that the guide must have had for him. Running a marathon is difficult enough, but to do it with somebody beside you, guiding them the entire way, is a huge sacrifice demonstrating love and respect. Not wanting to interrupt the team, I patiently ran behind them as I quietly observed how they worked in tandem.

This couple over in North Dakota, they were a bit different. The Bismarck marathon was a much smaller race than Chicago. We were out running in the country on the wide-open road. There weren't a lot of runners doing the full marathon, although there was a nice crowd for the 5K,

10K, and half marathon. With fewer runners to navigate around and fewer challenges on the course, there was less need for the constant guidance and verbal clues I'd seen in Chicago. The pair kept a physical closeness and held onto their ropes, and that seemed to be enough.

I watched them as we ran, imagining what they might be thinking and feeling. They had the biggest smiles on their faces. This blind man probably never thought he would ever run a marathon. With the help of his friend, he was doing something extraordinary! He was achieving something that he otherwise would never be able to do. I could see the look of joy and glee on his face. His gratitude for the experience made him glow. Runners often grunt, growl, and breathe heavily, their pained facial expressions showing their physical struggle. But this blind runner seemed to be experiencing joy in the journey. The look on his face and his body language told a story of contentment. The guide also had a huge smile. The woman seemed almost happier, knowing that she was helping this man achieve a goal that, without her, was out of his reach.

Guides. The most fortunate of us have guides throughout our lives. Our first guides are our parents, who carefully guide us away from dangers, like a fall down a flight of stairs. They may need to aggressively push us away from imminent peril, or they may gently wrap a strong arm around us and nudge us to safer ground. As we grow up, we eventually find guides outside our homes when, if we're lucky, we meet teachers who help us channel our ambitions in school and introduce us to subjects we love and even future career possibilities. Inspirational coaches and friends provide a depth of resources and help us through the difficult challenges life presents. Guides are driving forces in our growth and development at every stage, as long as we are open to their encouragement and advice.

The runner-guide relationships I've observed have caused me to think about how we navigate the world. In a deep and profound sense, we are all blind. We are all trying to make it through life, avoiding the potholes that can hurt us. We need friends and family who tell us when to jump over the curb so that we won't trip and fall on our faces. We need loving spouses and families who will stay right by our sides when the uphill climb starts and it's time to dig deep and push hard. We need voices of encouragement motivating us to the top. We need the comforting knowledge that we are safe in our struggle because they will be there by our side the whole way.

I've certainly appreciated guides during the uphill climbs in my life. New motherhood was terrifying to me, moving to new cities and states has been challenging, and balancing professional and family obligations requires a constant evaluation of priorities. At times I've needed someone close by, constantly telling me how to prepare for my next move, offering repetitive guidance, sometimes with every step I took.

In the quiet moments, I realize how blessed I've been by all the people in my life. The ones who hold the end of my rope, whispering those words of encouragement, helping me to do the unthinkable, to achieve heights I never dreamed were possible. Some guides have been quiet cheerleaders and encouragers, while others were more closely present. Life has required both types of guides. When I realize how important those people are in my life, it's humbling and inspiring. Each one of us has been on the receiving end of the rope. Each one of us has felt that need for help from another human being. Each one of us could point to people without whom we could not have achieved our goals. And each one of us has had the opportunity to hold the rope for others, the chance to feel the joy of being an instrument in helping someone else reach new heights.

As I ponder the guides in my life, past and present, I am left with new questions. Have I expressed gratitude to those who have guided me? Have I shown appreciation for the kind words of encouragement and let them know that they made a difference? And, what am I doing for other people? As we are guided by mentors, it then becomes our responsibility to mentor others. Could I do a little more to serve, inspire, and help those around me? Have I expressed joy for the opportunity to be someone's guide, a spectator on the front lines of her success?

Blindness. Literal blindness appeared to have affected this man from birth, but other types of blindness affect many of us. If we are blind to the guides in our lives, and blind to opportunities to be a guide for someone else, we go through life not recognizing the importance of one another. As the runners in North Dakota illustrated so profoundly to me, the simplest form of joy is when we run hand in hand, helping each other along the way.

FREEDOM

"If you want to live a happy life, tie it to a goal, not to people or objects."

—*Albert Einstein*

Part of having an ideal childhood is being sheltered from all the evil and dangers of the world. My sisters, brother, and I roamed backcountry roads on our bikes, never concerned about potential crime. We created problems with our own concocted shenanigans, but even that was harmless fun. Just the typical mischief kids engage in while flexing muscles during adolescence. We jumped from the roof of our home onto the trampoline and drove the family car on the dirt roads underage and unlicensed. Our childhood allowed us the freedom to explore our surroundings while figuring out the world we lived in. It was a wonderful foundation to build upon as I grew up, graduated high school, went to college, and became an adult.

The year I finished college, I graduated in late May and started working at my first real professional job. I felt like I was on top of the world having conquered college at a breakneck pace by taking maximum credits each semester, attending year-round, and then landing my first-choice job in the accounting department of one of the major employers in Boise, ID. Three months later, my world would turn upside down when terrorists attacked the Twin Towers on September 11th, 2001. The economy slowed down and I felt the burden and stress of being an adult with bills and obligations. I spent more time worrying about job security, finances, health, and safety, no longer recreating and spending my downtime in a carefree state of mind. I was shocked to learn that there were terrorist groups that would hurt innocent people to make a political statement against another country. I had understood war as it was taught in history books, but not this type of violence. My perspective was permanently altered and my assumption of safety was forever gone. I got a crash course on September 11th and continued to have my eyes opened during the following weeks, months, and years. My employer started regular layoffs and companies weren't hiring, increasing my stress. As a new college graduate, I knew I was still learning about corporate accounting and the business environment, not yet contributing as much as my more experienced peers. I worried about our macro economy and how that would affect me. I worried about my overall health and safety, and about my family. I worried more about everything and felt a constant undertone of stress flow through my life.

The attack on the Twin Towers was horrific and we've felt the effects as a country in each year that has followed. While this attack on my nation troubled me and permanently shifted the way I viewed the world, I would later experience a terrorist attack that would be more personal in nature when two men decided to detonate bombs near the finish line of the Boston Marathon. The bombs detonated at the finish line of the marathon—near the time I had finished and in the place I had been in a previous year. It was this attack that made me realize just how easily I could have been a casualty myself.

During lunch on a sunny April afternoon, my phone buzzed continuously with text and email notifications. I missed several calls before finally answering one from my brother. He sounded panicked and scared and asked where I was.

Me: "I'm at Subway."

Him (in an even more frantic tone): "You're on the subway?!"

Me: "Yeah, why?"

Him: "So you finished the race before the bombs went off?"

Me: "Zach, what are you talking about? I'm at Subway, not on the subway. I'm eating lunch."

Him: "Oh," he sighed audibly over the phone. "I thought you were on the subway in Boston. There was a terrorist attack in Boston. Several bombs went off and I was worried that you might have been there. They would have gone off about the time you would have finished."

My hands became too weak to hold my sandwich and I immediately felt nauseous. My heart raced. I was in shock. My friends were at Boston, my best friends. They had wanted me to join them, but because Easter was the day before the race, I had decided to skip running Boston to celebrate the holiday with my family. I felt angry and scared, not knowing if they were okay. My heart ached for those who were affected by the bombs.

On September 11 when the airplane struck the first Twin Tower, there was confusion as to whether it was an accident or an attack. Once the second airplane hit the second tower, all ambiguity was removed. We later found out about the other airplanes and the targets they had been headed for. As I heard about the bombs at the Boston Marathon finish line, I couldn't help but wonder what else was going to happen. Was this the first in a string of events? Were there going to be copycats at other large races? Who did this and why? What statement were they trying to make? Who would hurt innocent people running a race and spectating? It didn't make sense to me and I felt so violated. Terrorist attacks are senseless and confusing in general, but as a runner and marathoner, this felt more personal, directly connected to my everyday life. Running symbolized freedom to me. Being able to step outside my front door and let my stress and worries melt away as my feet pounded the pavement was liberating. Now I began to take precautions as I signed up for races. I considered the size of the city, if it was a point of interest, the size of the crowd, and if there might be a motive for a political statement in trying to harm participants. I chose not to participate in big races, particularly those sponsored by branches of the government like the Marine Corps Marathon. The NYC, Boston, Chicago, and Vegas marathons would have to wait for another time when I felt more safe. Instead of running being my release, I started to feel like a prisoner to fear.

I was a mother of four beautiful, smart, and very small children who will always be my first priority. Marathon running was a hobby. Now I found myself wondering if I should continue running marathons at all. Would something like the attack in Boston happen again at some other race and rob my children of their mother? My goal of running a marathon in each state wasn't worth leaving my children motherless.

The Boston Marathon bombing was in April. I was registered to run a marathon in June and had already booked my flight, hotel, and rental car. Still, I had a little bit of time to decide if I was going to continue on this journey or put it on the shelf until my children were older.

I wasn't alone in this worry. A tense and uneasy feeling was pervasive in the running community. While some people felt empowered by continuing to race, there were others who were scared. Some chose to avoid big races and opt for the smaller marathons that don't even attract a crowd at the finish line. Some chose to avoid racing all together. These were personal decisions based on personal comfort levels. I identified with aspects of all of the arguments. I wasn't sure what I was comfortable with.

Of my good friends who had raced in Boston that day, one in particular had narrowly escaped the bombing. She finished just minutes before the bombs went off and was just far enough from the finish line that she was unaffected. Had she taken a small walk break, a bathroom break, or had any disruptions to her usual pace, she could easily have been a casualty. When I began to wonder if running marathons was now too risky and if I should delay my racing ambitions until my family was raised, it was this friend who encouraged me to keep racing. If I altered my behavior, the terrorists would win. My friend offered to accompany me to my next marathon so we could move past this horrible tragedy together.

It wasn't easy. That June as I ran Grandma's Marathon in Duluth, Minnesota, I had an uneasy feeling. I felt myself looking at the racecourse with different eyes. Instead of looking for potholes that would twist my ankles, I looked for suspicious people lingering along the sidelines. I ran faster when I saw crowds because I knew spectators are a target for these types of attacks. My mind scrambled to identify potential dangers. Did the race water have anthrax in it? Any marathon puts stress on the mind and the body, but the heightened awareness of my dependency on others for hydration and nutrition made me realize how quickly something could go terribly wrong. I also depended on others to keep me safe, like the crossing guards and volunteers who directed me around the racecourse.

It was a rainy day and the misty weather disguised my tears. I cried for the loss of innocence. I cried because I felt robbed of peace of mind. I was no longer carefree and I mourned that loss. I cried because I knew the terrorists had forever changed the running community. I cried for those injured and their families. I cried because I didn't know what kind of a world I would release my children into. My heart felt heavy.

Before all this happened, my favorite thing was running down the hill in my neighborhood and following the trail as far as I wanted. I had taken my safety in doing this for granted, I realized later. My town is small and dozy, wonderfully sheltered from violence and crime. I sought a protected community to raise my family in so I could put my guard down and enjoy life. While running, the wind will breeze through my hair and I feel so free I'm sometimes even euphoric, practically floating along the path. The sunshine, the wind, the snow and rain, all of it makes me feel alive. Even on the days when I struggle to find the energy to run, there is an undertone of gratitude that my body allows me to enjoy being outdoors. This is my home, surrounded by nature, and I'd always felt safe in it.

After the bombing in Boston, I struggled as I evaluated my assumptions. I had taken so much for granted. Running had been my escape from stress. It was an activity I could do by myself that made me a better mother, friend, and person. I could let all my barriers down and just be myself, without worry. This fundamental enjoyment I derived from running was in jeopardy.

Step by step, my friend and I ran beside each other. We didn't talk like we usually do. We both retreated to a quiet, solemn place and pondered those who were affected at Boston. It was comforting to have her there, a security blanket as we traveled this new territory together.

As I finished the marathon, I was physically exhausted. I collected my medal, wrapped myself in a Mylar sheet, and sat on a rock near the post-race party. My friend joined me. We sat with our arms around one another and cried.

As we sat, I saw security guards on patrol. I looked down the final stretch of road leading to the finish and for the first time noticed that cement barricades had been placed along the route to prevent people from getting too close to the runners. I cried some more. What had happened to my sport? One of the best parts of running a marathon is seeing the crowds of people cheering the runners who are trying to dig deep and find the energy for the final stretch. The spectators cheer for all the runners with posters, cowbells, and horns, the cheers propelling runners to the finish line as small children beg for high fives. But this race was different. No one was there. The finish was void of encouragement. It felt like walking into your home, expecting a warm and familiar welcome, only to find it completely empty.

Since that initial marathon after the bombings, I've considered the small details of life that are so often taken for granted. That assumption of freedom we start to build our lives upon as children. The safety I had enjoyed throughout my life was now questioned. I felt vulnerable and raw. After

I exhausted myself crying that day I felt empty to my core. I was left with nothing in my soul but gratitude for the freedoms I continue to enjoy. I have a healthy body, I live in a safe town, I have my loved ones close, and I have access to healthy food, great health care, and cutting-edge technology. In that moment I prayed that I would never again take any of them for granted. Behind gratitude is awareness. When an event like the bombings occurs, it forces us to look at those little details we blissfully overlooked in more innocent days. I took inventory of all the details in my life that still allowed me to be free. So many blessings still enriched my life, and I have a lot to be grateful for.

Terrorist attacks can change people. They can make us angry. They can make us bitter toward religions and ethnicities. They can make us change our behavior and live fearfully. But they can also change us for the better. I resolved that I was not going to let one action change my behavior. I had spent over a decade on the roads enjoying my freedom. I'd traveled to countless races and encountered friendly and helpful people all along the way. I enjoy meeting people from different regions and religions. I enjoy understanding what motivates them. In understanding others, we begin to find similarities and can then begin to build relationships. I believe that most people are good and, for the most part, we all want the best for our families and communities. I choose to believe this even though there might be an occasion where that doesn't hold true. I resolved to focus on the blessings that make my world wonderful. By far, the good outweighs the bad.

The running community became strong. I was inspired at others' courage to continue, despite trepidation and fear. The security at large races has increased. The bag check process is permanently altered. The finish line crowds are patrolled. Racing will never be the same. But, the spirit of the marathon and the childlike feeling of elation a race brings are things that can't be taken away. They live inside each runner's soul, and terrorists can't destroy the human heart.

BOUNDARIES

"The future belongs to those who believe in the beauty of their dreams."

—*Eleanor Roosevelt*

One of the first words a toddler will learn and repeat is "no." They get used to hearing that word as they head for the stairs on their wobbly little fat legs. When they reach to stick their finger into the light socket, a frantic parent will sharply scream "Nooooooo!" As a small child goes to retrieve a ball out of the middle of the road, adults will again yell in an effort to keep their child safe. We draw boundaries of safety in order for our children to flourish. We want to help them avoid pain, discomfort, unhappiness, and danger. As children grow up, they become able to identify potential dangers themselves, without needing adults to constantly remind them. As parents, we anticipate this time and take a collective sigh of relief when it finally arrives. At last we can let our hair down and relax without scanning every new situation for potential threats.

Through our watchfulness, we have inadvertently instilled a fear of the unknown into our children. We have taught them that if a situation is a little hard, dangerous, or unfamiliar it should be avoided. If our children are wise, they will approach new environments and situations with heaps of skepticism. As we set boundaries to keep them safe, we also send a message that they should be scared of the unknown and cautious when trying something new. We send mixed messages about approaching new challenges that take us out of our comfort zones. However, without challenging experiences that force growth, personal development is stunted.

Boundaries can be placed upon us by our environment or by other people, but the most dangerous boundaries are those we set around ourselves. We too often set boundaries that are confining, choosing not to push ourselves beyond our perceived limits.

One of my first experiences being pushed past my limits happened when I was about 14 years old. My parents thought it would be a good idea for me to participate in 4-H by taking responsibility for my own steer. Since my dad operated a cattle ranch with several thousand head of cattle, we had easy access to the steer, food, vaccinations, housing, and labor for the steer. Dad agreed to have his hired help do all the daily work, but it was my responsibility to tame the steer. Cattle are naturally frightened of people, so the first step would be to spend enough time with my large furry friend so he wouldn't jump and run every time I got close to him. After we got used to each other, I would need to put a harness on him and teach him to walk beside me, starting and stopping when I wanted. In 4-H, steers would be judged based on their quality (how well they were cared for) and showmanship (how well they were trained).

My dad's ancestors had been raising steers for generations and had perfected the process of feeding and caring for the animals. My dad knew just the right balance of alfalfa, corn, grain, etc. to feed the steers so the perfect amount of fat was marbled into the meat. The quality of the steer would be the easy part, especially since I didn't have to do any of it. The other piece of the puzzle, my contribution, terrified me. But in my family, being terrified wasn't ever a good reason to shy away from a challenge. I protested my participation in 4-H, but my father is a firm man and he had made up his mind. I would be entering a steer in the county fair.

The steer may have been afraid of me, but I was more afraid of it, scared even to go near the large beast. I preferred my steers to be in front of me on a plate, well done, and next to a pile of A-1 sauce. Not alive. And certainly not where they could hit me with their heads or kick me. My heart pounded and my hands shook each time I went to work with my steer. My brother, the kindest person I know, would run my steer through the vaccination chute (a narrow path where the steer is trapped) and harness him for me. He would tie the steer to the corral post it couldn't escape. Over the first weeks and months of summer, I would offer the steer fresh-cut hay from the stack and talk to him like we were friends. I figured we would be spending a lot of time together, and we might as well get acquainted. Talking to him made me feel calmer. Little did I know, talking to someone who couldn't understand or talk back was perfect training for years later, when I'd be a mother of four children.

Eventually, the time came to take my steer for a walk and teach him how to show in the county fair. I had picked out the steer in the early spring. Now that summer was here, I only had a few months until the fair and I knew I needed to get my steer trained to show. We weren't deathly afraid of each other by now, although I was still quite nervous around this animal. I know that animals react on instincts. And as much as humans like to think they have control over animals, I maintain a healthy respect for animal instincts. My steer weighed in around 900 pounds and would grow to over 1,200 pounds from spring to the end of summer. I, conversely, weighed 110 pounds and thankfully didn't grow at the same rate as my steer. As I tried to lead the steer, I would push and pull on the harness. I put every pound I had into that rope, trying to get him to comply. Nothing worked. I feared aggravating him, that he would ram me with his head or kick me.

All the while, I still did not want to do this 4-H project, but as I mentioned, it was my dad's idea and he was making me do it. My dad resembles Gaston from Beauty and the Beast. He is a huge man with bulging muscles as solid as pieces of steel. As he has aged, his hair has turned white and he wears reading glasses, but his muscles remain the same as when he was in his 20s. Dad's arms were as big as my upper thighs and his legs as big as my waist. Though he's a monster of a man, he has a soft spot for his children.

I knew what I had to do. I ran crying to my dad. I pled my case and begged to quit. I was not cut out for this task and I could not do it, no matter how hard I tried. Dad gave me a hug, took my hand, and walked me back to the corral. He told me to sit and watch. Dad grabbed the rope attached to the harness and, with a firm jerk, led that steer around the corral until the steer realized that it was in his best interest to follow the leader.

After Dad walked the steer, the steer let his stubborn streak disappear. Dad would hand me the rope and tell me that it was my turn. We did this for weeks until my steer no longer needed to be broken in first by my dad. Before I knew it, the summer was nearing an end. As I made my final preparations for the fair, I realized that, with my dad's help, I was now able to do something that had seemed impossible mere months earlier.

During the show at the fair, I was still unsure of how my steer would act. Loud clapping or a child's shrieks could startle it and make it act irrationally. Plus, my steer was kept at the fair and anyone could come by and interact with him. All of this increased my nervousness. During the show, my whole body was filled with anxiety and I shook uncontrollably. Decades later, I feel a familiar wave of panic just recalling the experience. The cattle judge had us complete various showing techniques so he could see who had done the best job. The judge then ranked the showmen from the top to the bottom. First place is labeled quality and second is reserve. From there on down, the number system was employed. I hoped I wouldn't be last, but understood if I was. Mostly I was just glad that at the end of the show I would no longer have to deal with this steer.

The judge awarded the quality ranking to my brother. I was so happy for him! We all grew up on the farm, but he spent more time working there from a young age. Driving a tractor at six years old and buying cattle at the auction at eight, he was and still is a natural on the farm. As the judge walked by, I was curious to see who would be awarded reserve prize. He walked past me and as my eyes followed him, he turned around and pointed back to me. I was reserve showman!

Shocked and speechless, I felt the most amazing wave of happiness spread throughout my body. I did it! Not by myself, but I still did it! I worked with my steer and overcame my fears. Not only that, but I had accomplished the task with high honors. If I approached life's challenges in a similar manner, I could do anything. The immediate sense of satisfaction gave way to a boost in confidence. I had gone from unwilling and terrified to successful and confident within six months of trying something outside of my comfort zone.

Over 15 years later, I would be faced with another experience that would push me out of my comfort zone. I somehow had convinced myself that it would be extremely difficult to run a marathon. Running 26.2 miles seemed impossible! I think I suffer from a mild form of adult ADD because I get restless when I've been doing anything non-engaging for long periods of time. I get bored driving for 26.2 miles. Certainly I could never complete 26.2 miles running without getting bored out of my mind or collapsing in a heap of exhausted flesh at the end. The best-case scenario, I was convinced, would have me as the last person to finally roll (or crawl) across the finish line just as the race cutoff time approached. To that point, I had never been a serious runner, and I felt a sense of uncertainty when I told friends and family my lofty goal. But there was some magical appeal to the idea of running a marathon. Once I thought about the possibility, I couldn't get it out of my head. While I was terrified of trying and failing, I wanted to see what it would feel like to cross the finish line. The balancing act of fear and curiosity kept teetering back and forth, and I eventually committed to run the race.

I had been running consistently for about nine months. Having just graduated college with my accounting degree and starting my first professional job, I was ready for my next goal. It was the fall of 2002 and I had just enrolled at Boise State University in the Master's of Tax program. I needed a physical outlet to relieve stress from my job and school. Running experts recommend that to successfully train for a marathon, one should have at least a year of consistent running and a base of 40-45 miles for weekly mileage. Without telling anyone, over the next year I slowly built up my weekly mileage, while devouring every piece of information I could get about the marathon through books, magazines, and the internet. I was obsessed with learning how to run a marathon successfully. I continued to train and gather information to help ease my nerves in my newfound adventure.

The first time I ran 10 miles, I was so proud of myself: I had finally reached double digits! I realized that if I slowly increased my long run and my weekly mileage, I wasn't going to be doing anything that much harder than what I had already accomplished. This rationalization helped calm my nerves. Once I wrapped my head around the idea of running a certain distance, my legs, body, and heart just did what my head told them to. Even as my runs grew much longer, my body completed the task at hand.

While I remained nervous and scared, the more information I gathered and the more training I completed, the more my fears subsided. At last, I found a race that was out of town (I didn't want to embarrass myself by failing in front of my friends in my hometown community!) and decided to sign up. I knew I would never feel completely ready, but that if I had a date and a distance to work toward, I would be more likely to stick to a training plan and actually run the race.

The marathon I'd found was in late September and started in the mountains of Logan Canyon. It was the perfect time of the year, with crisp morning air that would warm up in the afternoon. The race started early and I projected that I should be finished before it got too warm. I knew and loved the Rocky Mountains; they were the backdrop of my childhood. I felt comforted by the familiar location of my first race and was very excited.

I didn't want to put pressure on myself to qualify for the Boston Marathon on my first marathon, but I couldn't help but think about it. I knew that most people work hard to achieve that level of success and I would be greedy to expect it the first time, especially after becoming a serious runner less than a year ago. I'd run a half marathon about six months after I'd started running regularly, and that was my longest race to date. The learning curve was still steep. Running experts generally agree that the best way to approach a race is to have three levels of goals: a best-case scenario, a realistic goal, and a worst-case scenario. At the very least (worst case), I wanted to finish—and not be the last person to finish. As a realistic goal I wanted to finish in less than four hours. Best-case scenario would be qualifying for Boston.

I didn't sleep very much in the days leading up to the marathon. I didn't eat well, either. I was so overcome with nerves that I could barely think of anything else. The race couldn't come fast enough, yet I almost dreaded it! When race day finally arrived, I rode the bus to the start at the top of the mountain. It was still dark outside and the ride seemed to take forever. All I could think was that if it took that long to get to the top, it would take so much longer to get to the bottom.

Before long, we had started the race and I was on my way. To qualify for the Boston Marathon, I would need to finish in three hours and 40 minutes. The miles went by and I felt great————but I knew that I'd feel strong for the first few miles. I was more nervous about the last six miles, which would be new territory. My focus at the beginning of the race was to resist the urge to go too fast. As I passed the six-mile mark, I knew I was about 25%

done. I felt strong and optimistic. The miles slowly passed and I approached the half marathon mark. I was still feeling strong and my pace was steady. I enjoyed the beautiful scenery, the music I was listening to, and running alongside other people. Aside from my half marathon, I trained solo. Having others around was a nice change. I saw their running form, their gadgets (and made a mental note to look them up on the internet when I got home), and their clothing. The cheering spectators were also a fun distraction. Cute little children handed out orange slices and asked for high fives. People rang cowbells, held up witty posters, and cheered for every runner as they passed. Their enthusiasm fueled me as I ran mile after mile.

After the half marathon point, I started approaching magic mile 20. Mile 20 is known as "the wall" in most running circles. Most plans don't have runners train past 20 miles, and it's in those last six miles that the body and the mind have their final battle. The body will be fatigued and mentally most runners are ready to be done. When I reached this point, I knew I had to keep pushing. My hamstrings were tight from running downhill for the last 20 miles and I decided to stop and stretch at a water station. I glanced at my watch and noticed that I was not only on target to qualify for Boston, but I had time to spare. This realization gave me a jolt of energy. My mind and my body began negotiations. My mind told my body that if it ran another mile, I could stop briefly to stretch my calves, hips, and hamstrings. For the next six miles, I ran and stretched repeatedly. And then I had finally made it to mile 26. I was so close now that I knew I would not fail. Based on the time, I also knew I was going to qualify for Boston. Again, I felt a jolt of energy shoot through my body. As I ran past the timing mats, I saw the finish time's neon yellow numbers shining back at me. I finished my first marathon with the final time of 3:33:33.

I hadn't ever been a runner and didn't have much confidence going into this new adventure. As I ran the marathon, I was next to people who were lifelong runners with mounds of knowledge. I felt so insecure in my ignorance. I didn't want to fail, and didn't want to fail publically either. But, there was something about the allure of trying that appealed to me. I had pushed myself outside of the boundaries I had created in my head. I finished strong, I qualified for Boston—I did it! I did something that terrified me, that I didn't think I could do. I had worked so hard. A lump in the back of my throat started to grow until I could hardly breathe. Tears rolled down my cheeks as I crossed the line.

When our parents give us boundaries, they do it to keep us safe. But sometimes those boundaries convince us that we shouldn't try something new or hard. And sometimes we need to break through those boundaries to make new boundaries for ourselves. As I blasted through the boundary of not believing I was capable of running 26.2 miles, let alone qualifying for one of the most prestigious road races, I questioned other boundaries I had placed on myself. I reconsidered my education, my profession, my personal growth and development. Every aspect in my life was now going to be examined. I made myself a promise that I wasn't going to live my life inside the boundaries.

When my first gut instinct is to say "I can't" and come up with a list of all the reasons something would be difficult, I promised myself that instead I would say "I can" or "I will try."

I was not always a runner. Until now, I have never written a book. I am not a natural cook. Before having kids, I hadn't spent much time around small children. There are a lot of things I have never done. And a lot of them scare me. I am afraid of failing, privately and publically. However, having experienced the satisfaction that comes from trying—not even necessarily succeeding—I resolved to try more. I found myself skiing down black diamonds that looked too steep. I found myself learning to surf at 36 years old. I have four children and I am writing a book. I still can't cook very well, but I have learned how to make food good enough to keep my family alive. I don't succeed at everything, but I do my best. I try.

This paradigm shift in my attitude has been one of the most empowering attributes I have gained through running. I lost a lot in committing to becoming a runner. I lost sleep. I've lost late night movie outings with friends. I've lost the opportunity to have spare time to explore other hobbies. But I have gained so much more. I have gained a lens through which I am able to internalize and process life. I gained confidence that I can do anything I want to. I became kind to myself, knowing when to push and when to rest. I've learned to love my body for what it IS, instead of not liking for what it ISN'T. I gained respect for myself. I've gained everything important and lost beliefs that held me back.

Over the last decade, I have gathered inspiration from some individuals I admire. James Lawrence is a Guinness World Record holder and he inspired me with his idea that no dream is too big. Eleanor Roosevelt's words that encourage others to try something new every day have also inspired me. If I start approaching life's challenges with a "why not" attitude instead of "why," I knew I wouldn't be a spectator in life, I would be an active participant.

Three years after my first marathon, I committed myself to running a marathon in all 50 states. And as I made that commitment I channeled these ideas. I knew it was a big dream. I knew that as I traveled to different states and ran the marathons, there would be opportunities for me to grow and that I would need to pace myself to ensure that I kept the bigger picture in sight. And I knew it was worth it to try. And so I encourage you: Try it! Dream a goal that is BIG and try something new. It's liberating, and it feels amazing to not have chains and boundaries holding you back.

While success feels exhilarating, this process hasn't been void of failure. I have had to scrape myself off the ground, literally, and dig to the very depths of my soul to push through challenges. Failure can often be a better teacher than success. Either way, there is a lesson to be learned. It's not about the finish line, it's about the process.

FEAR

"Success is not final, failure is not fatal: it is the courage to continue that counts."

—*Winston Churchill*

Being eaten by a cougar is my biggest fear when I'm out for a morning run. Cougars are native to the Northwest. They live mostly in solitude and will roam a territory of 25-30 miles stalking prey when they are in need of nourishment. Though there is some variation, most cougars are about the size of an adult human. They are called "ambush predators" because they prefer to hide in tall grass, shrubs, and trees, waiting for prey to pass by before attacking and devouring the meat from its bones. Cougars prefer to feed in the wee morning hours, right before the sun comes up. Deer are their main source of food because they are larger than bush animals, making them easier targets. Deer have tails that are highly visible when they bound through tall grass. When my runner friends and I pull our hair back in ponytails for our early morning runs, I know our swishing hair resembles deer's tails. We are potential prey. I am acutely aware of the dangers running on the trails through the mountains of Washington.

Perhaps it's my imagined visual of being eaten by a cougar that escalates this fear into a phobia—an irrational fear. By definition, one can't logically rationalize a phobia away. I know the statistics are in my favor and that I have a very low chance of actually being eaten by a cougar. I will probably never even see one. However, simply knowing that cougars live in the mountains, that they are hungry, and that I would make a nice meal makes this phobia a realistic fear.

Cougars aren't the only forms of wildlife to be wary of while running in the great outdoors. There are coyote, foxes, wolves, snakes, porcupines, raccoons, skunks, and even neighborhood dogs that at times can seem more scary than the unknown animals making noises in the shrubbery. But while most wildlife is more afraid of humans than we are of it, the difference for me is that cougars are unpredictable—and have very large claws and teeth. And if I learned anything from "Little Red Riding Hood," it's that those large claws and teeth would be better to eat me with. The concept seems to apply to cougars just as well as big, bad wolves.

When I signed up for the Anchorage, Alaska, marathon my biggest fear was not cougars, but the bears. My dad takes an annual guys' fishing trip to Alaska and has had a few close encounters with these large beasts. Many of his pictures from these trips have bears in the background. I knew I could very possibly encounter one myself, and I felt very nervous to be running 26.2 miles through their territory.

Studying the course map, I learned that the marathon would begin in downtown Anchorage before guiding us onto the Tony Knowles trail, a lovely paved pedestrian path that curves along the waterfront. The trail winds through remote areas where foot traffic is rare. Alaska is home to one of the largest rainforests in North America. Spread over 17 million acres, the Tongass National Forest stretches along the southeastern part of the Alaskan panhandle. Average rainfall varies between 26 and 162 inches, making for a very wet climate. Anchorage, located along the rainforest, is green, lush, and humid. Along the banks of the water the vegetation is so thick you can't see a foot into the trees and plants. It would be impossible to see a potential threat lurking there. If I were to encounter a bear, I'd likely come across it alone, with little to no advance warning.

Still, for at least some of the race I'd be among other runners, and I had a finely-honed strategy from training back home. As I had with my running friends in the early mornings when cougars might be looking for breakfast— a fear my running friends found ridiculous—I hedged my bets. Self-preservation was the name of the game. When there were other runners nearby, I stayed to their left, putting them as a barrier between the shrubs and myself as I hugged the coastal side of the trail. These poor victims would be the low-hanging fruit for any hungry bear to pick off. I, being an additional three feet away, would be harder to catch to eat. Plus, on the safer coastal edge of the trail, if a bear charged I could protect myself by quickly grabbing the other person and offering them as a human sacrifice before I ran off down the nearest hill.

I had a plan and an ironclad backup plan. Human lives might be sacrificed, but they wouldn't include mine. I was ready to visit the great state of Alaska and face my fears.

The race began, and I ran swiftly. At first I kept to my plan, sticking close to other runners. By the middle of a marathon, though, I often find myself getting lost in the miles. In races I tend to notice major mile markers, like the half marathon point or a turnaround point. I will remember breathtaking scenery. At times, I will remember other runners. But generally, I let my mind meander, not paying close attention to my surroundings. Somewhere mid-race, I let down my guard. We had looped around, and I knew that I was on the final stretch heading back toward downtown. With the race going well and the more obscure parts of the trail behind me, my mind was at ease.

And then, rounding the corner, I saw them. In front of me were a huge female moose and her baby calf, drinking from a stream mere feet away.

All along I had planned my escape from a potential bear attack. I hadn't done my homework on how to escape from a moose, and a mother moose at that, one I quickly realized would be even worse because they are known to be very aggressive in protecting their young. Luckily, neither mother nor baby had noticed me.

To my left I saw a bank of shrubs, trees, and other greenery. To my right was the small creek the moose and her calf were drinking from. They blocked the path with their large bodies. I would need to step off the path and into the shrubs to get around the moose. I slowed to a tip-toe. My mind went blank. My once fast and strong legs became weak and heavy. I didn't know what to do. I needed to get past this moose and to a safe place. I knew that the moose could charge at any time and I could be trampled. I could get seriously hurt. I could even die.

There was only one thing to do: creep behind Mrs. Moose as quietly as possible. I hoped, if I made any noise, that she would assume I was just a little squirrel, bounding around in nature minding my own business, and pay no attention.

My heart was beating out of my chest and the blood drained to the bottom of my feet. I ran as quickly and quietly as I ever had in my entire life. Once past the moose, I continued on the trail alongside the stream as fast as I could run. Miles later, I finally gathered the courage to look behind me and see if I had any followers. Much to my relief, I saw nothing but trail and trees.

Sometimes I have to laugh at my fears, knowing how unrealistic and silly they are, and how differently things play out than we expect. I had feared cougars and bears. I had prepared for them. In the end, I faced something different, something that had never occurred to me. Rarely do our worst-case scenarios play out exactly as we anticipate. Rarely do our biggest fears become reality.

I used to have a phobia of flying. While I knew that there are more vehicle deaths than airplane deaths, I still didn't like the idea. The concept of thousands of pounds of steel floating in the air amazes me. I understood the mechanics, yet it still seemed impossible that airplanes stayed in the sky! One day, I was convinced, the laws of science would no longer apply. The airplane would drop, and I would die. In the airport, I'd make peace with my maker, certain of my imminent death. After boarding each flight, my palms would sweat and my body would shake. I would try to distract myself by talking to the person next to me. Turbulence was the worst; I was certain with every bump that the plane was going down. I would arrive safely at my destination, exhausted from anxiety, white knuckles still clenching the armrests.

It wasn't until I became a mother that I finally got comfortable with flying. Distracted with taking care of my small children I was simply too busy to dwell on the possibility of my imminent death. During the flight, the more I helped my kids be calm, the calmer I was myself. As time has gone on, I've realized how silly my phobia was. Sure, planes do crash and people have died. But the likelihood of me being injured from an airplane ride is so remote that my many hours imagining it were just a waste of time.

We can let our fears control us and modify our behaviors. Sometimes our fears prevent us from experiencing life's most enriching lessons. In running marathons, I have faced a lot of fears. Fear of not finishing. Fear of what it will take to run a PR. Fear of setting high goals and not reaching them. Fear of telling friends my wildest dreams and not reaching them. Fear. It is an emotion that limits us from doing what we are capable of.

Worry often goes along with fear. I still find myself worrying about unlikely events.

Motherhood brought out my worrying side. Mostly, I worried that I would be a horrible parent. I hadn't even changed a diaper before I had my first baby! I didn't know how to burp them and the idea of cleaning up vomit made me queasy. How do you teach a baby how to roll over, use the potty, or speak? All of these were markings of a good mother, according to coffee shop chatter. I was doomed to be a failure because of my inexperience! I didn't even need to worry about how to teach a kid to tie a shoe or ride a bike because I would be deemed a lost cause long before that time came.

As my kids grew, I worried over every milestone. Now that they're out of babyhood, I worry about each decision I make and its potential consequences. I worry as I think about the future, when my kids will be driving, dating, going off to college and living on their own, possibly marrying and having their own families. I worry when I watch the news and hear about school shootings, kidnappings, rapes, car accidents, and all the various dangers that are part of living.

For the most part, these fears haven't played out. But other things have. One of my kids ate a handful of sand. One bombed a spelling test. Not one of my four children was potty trained before their third birthday. My kids are not the top students in their class or the best athletes on the field. My daughter rarely went a day in the first two years of her schooling without turning a discipline card. She also once kicked the doctor in the face when he leaned in to look at a wart on her finger. Despite my frequent and regular protests, one of my children spent his first three years with a finger up his nose. I think my kids all brush their teeth every day, but their breath sometimes tells another story. Some of these are minor failures, but at times they've seemed to confirm my worst fears: I was a bad mother.

Yet, I have learned that fearing how the overall development of my children is going based on these minor failures is silly. Worrying about the small stuff isn't important. I am not a bad mother. My children are loved, healthy, and happy.

My marathon in Alaska is a reminder that not every fear, founded or unfounded, will come to fruition. While I can do my best to prepare for the worst-case scenarios, life will hand me different challenges I am not expecting. And that's okay. Whatever happens, I will make the best decision I am able to at the time. Whether I'm thinking about a moose or a finger up the nose, I've learned that I need to spend less time bracing for life's potential challenges, and simply face the ones that actually come.

CHALLENGES

"We know what we are, but know not what we may be"

—*William Shakespeare*

I feel the vibration of my alarm clock. I reach under my pillow, where I always stow away the clock so the sound only wakes me, allowing the little bodies that found their way to my side in the middle of the night to remain asleep. I turn off my alarm and quietly slip out of the sheets and tiptoe to the bathroom to get dressed for my morning run. The night before, as usual, I set out my running clothes. It is much easier to set out my clothing than to think about anything in the early morning hours. Once dressed, I sneak away from my warm and cozy bedroom to explore, to think, and to just be.

Running is my escape from the mundane. I started running in college while getting my MBA when group projects, midterms, finals, and papers filled my schedule. Life at the time was so dynamic, fun, and exciting. Running brought something constant, the stability I needed to have mental peace. I ran to bring balance to my life and to have quiet time to think through the major decisions that seemed never-ending.

After college was marriage, another life change. Running reminded me that although I was married, I was still my own individual. I loved having my own hobbies and maintaining my own identity, something that was just mine, that I didn't have to justify, explain, or share with anyone.

I started working in a corporate office after graduating with my accounting degree and tried to balance the demands of family and work life. Being an adult with responsibilities was a drastic change from college life and again, I craved balance.

Children came along several years after, slowly chipping away at my personal time. I still run in search of the balance of maintaining individuality and being part of a marriage, family, and community. At times, I feel myself giving in to conformity, and I fight against that urge. I run to remind myself that somewhere inside is a girl I used to know. I want to make sure I don't forget her, that she isn't hidden under the responsibilities of life. I run to remember that while the world may try to tell me what kind of person to be, how to be a supportive wife and an effective mother, inside I know the truth. When I spend time with myself, I find that I don't need the world to tell me what or who to be. The girl I know, my inner self, helps me find the answers to the questions life constantly presents. Running helps me find myself when I start to feel lost.

Lost. There have been times in my life when I have felt profoundly lost. When I was alone and everywhere I looked was scary and unfamiliar. I have felt a deep empty feeling that no amount of running, shopping, and busyness could fill. And here I sit now, once again, feeling quite lost. There is a change on my horizon that has left me feeling scared, terrified even—a move to a new city several hours away. I feel my soul retracting into a deep corner of my body, not wanting to engage with friends or family. Knowing that I have a limited amount of time left to enjoy friends and activities in my home of over a decade, I try to make use of what little remains. However, every encounter with friends and local activity reminds me that one more thing I currently enjoy will soon be gone. And somewhere in all these changes, I realize I have lost myself.

Material items are easily replaced with newer and nicer things. Homes can be bought, sold, and decorated. It takes a lot of effort to sift through the crowds to find a few good friends you can connect with, but with time, it will happen. Almost everything we spend our time and money and effort on can be replaced. Except oneself. One can't simply replace oneself. Lately I look inside myself to see any shred of the girl I used to know and I realize that she isn't there anymore.

This move is indicative of much more than putting my personal items into a box and finding a new house. I know that with time I will integrate into a new community, the kids will find friends at a new school, and within a year or two the memories of my current life will have faded into the background. So I mourn the loss of my wonderfully beautiful life as I know it. But on a much deeper level, I mourn the loss of myself. This move represents an awareness that somewhere along the way, my life stopped feeling like my own.

A job change for my husband is causing this move, the same reason I moved the time before. Perhaps if we were moving for a new, exciting opportunity for me, I would feel differently. I would have something to look forward to, lessening the pain of leaving behind a collection of dear friends. Instead, I see all the challenges I will face as I try to find a new neighborhood, school, church, dentist, and pediatrician for my family. Finding swim teams, soccer, piano teachers, grocery stores, health and fitness centers, shopping places, and all the tiny pieces of life that make me happy seems overwhelming. My anxiety is paralyzing at times, but I know that in time I will figure out all those details. In time I hope to be happy again. But now, I am just sad. I recall special memories in places, knowing that when I leave those memories will be in a past chapter of my life. I think of how the people here have touched me, knowing that I will drift apart from most of them. I think of all the happy memories I have made and feel like this piece of my life ended with the story still unfinished.

In marriage and in life there is a constant game of tug-of-war. I know that for my husband to further his career, I need to be willing and supportive of his dreams. And doing that will provide opportunities for our children. I want my husband and my children to be happy. I am hopeful that my unhappiness is temporary, but not knowing if my feelings are temporary or permanent causes me anxiety. I also feel like my world could be turned upside down again by another job relocation, which makes me reluctant to immerse myself in my new world. When all these factors are meshed together, I feel like I'm suffocating, lost in a haze of fog.

I frantically look for landmarks to guide me, to provide comfort and a sense of order. Faith and family are anchors in my life, and have given me clarity in approaching most problems. And friends, those carefully chosen soulmates, often act as anchors through rocky times. They sometimes know me better than I know myself. They have my best interests in mind, and know my thoughts without me needing to vocalize them. They know my strengths and weaknesses. My dear friends let me lean on them through the hard times.

But this time is different. My friends will stay and I will go. I am moving farther away from my family and won't see them as often. As much as I know we live in a connected world with social media, texting, phone calls, etc., it is still difficult to stay connected when life drifts further away. And so I reach out to my place of solace, my running shoes. They are the bridge that helps me leave my past life and journey to my new life. They help me feel less lost. They give me the time to rediscover myself. While my running shoes might occasionally get me lost, they are also what keeps me found. Without running, without the time it gives me to remember myself, I'm afraid I would remain lost.

Running has taught me that I can do hard things. I don't need to do them all at once. I just need to have the courage to lace up my shoes and take one step at a time. The step doesn't have to be big or fast. I can take tiny steps when that is all my body can handle. And with this move, I will take tiny steps. I will pack one box at a time. I will tackle the issues I feel ready and capable of handling. I will find a good school for my kids. I will find a comfortable house in a safe neighborhood. I will find the grocery stores with the fresh produce. I will find the dentist who is kind to my children and makes the experience enjoyable. I will eventually find friends who make me laugh until my stomach hurts. My new life won't replace what I am leaving behind, but it will still be enjoyable.

Learning how to push myself when I feel too tired and discouraged to continue will be an asset as I force myself to engage in my new life. I will keep pushing until I make it to the finish line. I might feel victorious. I might feel defeated. I don't know the ending, but I am still taking small steps forward. I know the girl in the running shoes can and will make it to the finish line. I have acquired grit, that never-ending perseverance that has taught me to succeed.

Moving will feel like another marathon. Each race is different and special in its own way. The cadence, speed, racecourse, and environment are each unique. They can be enjoyable without comparison. Running has taught me that this principle is true. As I look at my past and see how running has reminded me who I am and who I have always been, it also inspires me to look at the course ahead and realize that I will always be myself regardless of what life has waiting.

ASSUMPTIONS

"The best people possess a feeling for beauty, the
courage to take risks, the discipline to tell the truth,
the capacity for sacrifice. Ironically, their virtues
make them vulnerable; they are often wounded,
sometimes destroyed."

—*Ernest Hemingway*

I stood at the starting line of the Deseret News Classic Marathon in Salt Lake City, Utah, in late July. I hadn't been running for very long and it was only my fifth or sixth marathon. Still learning about marathoning and running, I was self-conscious about breaking any written or unwritten rules. One unwritten rule of race etiquette is about properly seeding yourself. For example, it is incredibly rude for someone who will run a 14-minute mile to start with those running a seven-minute mile. Everyone who runs faster than a 14-minute mile but slower than a seven-minute mile will need to run around that one person who started in the wrong spot. Constantly dodging people (or worse, whole groups of people) wastes a lot of time and energy. If everyone improperly seeded himself or herself, people would be bumping into each other and darting all over the racecourse. Minutes spent stuck behind other runners are not only extremely frustrating, but can also cost marathoners entries to time-qualified races.

Some of the larger races have pace groups. These are led by individuals who keep a steady pace over the course to allow other runners to run alongside them, without having to worry about their own time. Pacers do the hard work for you. You find the person who is holding a sign with your expected finish time and you stick with her or him the whole race. But if the race is smaller and pacers aren't available, you have to go about finding similar-paced runners the old-fashioned way. You glance to the front, right, left, and back to see what the other runners look like. If they look like you, you are in the right spot. If you are feeling social, you can ask your neighbor their anticipated finish to gauge your own seeding.

The Deseret News is a smaller race and didn't have pace groups. To seed myself that morning in Salt Lake City, I looked around, moving within the group of runners until the ones around me looked like they might run at my pace. I usually finish in the top five percent of overall runners. I never go just in front of the starting line, but I like to start close to the front. As I looked to my left I saw a vertically challenged girl. She must have been a foot and a half shorter than me. Her legs were muscular and strong, but weren't very long. I thought it would be nearly impossible for her to keep pace with the front of the pack. Her leg rotation would have to be 50% faster than any of the rest of ours! Judging by her exterior, she had grossly overestimated her abilities and was bound cause one of those bottlenecks every runner is annoyed by.

Maybe this was her first race? Maybe she didn't know the unwritten rules of seeding? I was a newer runner and was discovering this information through extensive reading. What would be a tactful way to help someone in this situation? Would it be tactful to say something? What would Dear Abby or Miss Manners advise? I've never been comfortable correcting others or telling them what to do, and though I debated, in the end I kept my thoughts to myself.

The gun went off and the gal shot out of the gate like a bullet. I've never seen such small legs with such a high turnover. Her blond French braids flew away, bobbing up and down until she disappeared from my line of vision. I never saw her again. I ran a great race and stayed on pace, but she was just faster. Everything I'd guessed about her was wrong. Yet making assumptions is so natural to do!

As much as I'd like to say that I learned my lesson and that I never judged another person after that, I made a similar mistake years later. It was November and I had been accepted as an elite runner in the New York Marathon. I had tried several times to get into this prestigious race, but my name was never picked in the lottery. Finally, in 2008, my dreams were about to come true. I had a golden ticket into the race I had been waiting years to run.

I gathered with 40,000 others to run through the five boroughs. New York is one of the largest races in not just the United States, but in the world. Runners travel from all over to participate, and the logistics of it left this farm girl wide-eyed. I'd never seen so many people run a single marathon. As the race drew nearer the energy in my body was electric.

When you register for this race, you put in your expected finish time and are given a starting position accordingly, eliminating the problem of people improperly seeding themselves. Because I had qualified with a fast finish at a half marathon, I had the option of starting in the front with the other elite runners, right behind the professionals who were expected to win the race. There were few public roads that could handle the sheer volume of runners, so marathoners began from three different starting locations. As the race progressed, we were eventually funneled down an eight-lane highway.

It was awesome to run elbow to elbow with my 40,000 new best friends. I saw heads bobbing as far as my eye could see. One of my running idols is Paula Radcliff, who was the women's world record holder for the fastest marathon time when I started running and whom I had tuned in to watch run in the Olympics. The critics blasted her for jerking her head around when she ran. Her form was unconventional and distracting, but she was undeniably a very talented runner. That day in New York, I spotted someone else who was moving his upper body side to side in a very strange manner. The more I watched the random guy, the more interesting he became. His stride, gait, and running form were nothing short of horrific. How was he keeping such a good pace?

The crowds were so thick, I could only see from his shoulders up to his head. Occasionally I would glance over at him swaying back and forth, in awe that he was able to keep up, given all the extra energy he was expending. As the miles went by, the crowds eventually spread out. It is always a happy moment when you get some distance from others. Runners can be a gross bunch. Aside from the stinky smell they usually omit, I have had people lean to the side and blow snot rockets without looking to see if there's another runner in their way. I have seen people spit without looking. One time, I saw a woman stop in the middle of the road and relieve herself. The chance to get away from other runners is one I never pass up.

As I moved to give myself more personal space, I saw the guy again. As his upper body swayed back and forth, the crowds had thinned enough that I could look down to see what his legs were doing. That's when I saw that he was a double amputee on running blades. Since he didn't have knees to bend, he was essentially leaning his upper body far enough to the side that he could swing his opposite prosthetic around to the front of his body, then repeat the same motion on the opposite side. I watched him keep pace with me, swinging his legs and using the momentum of his body to keep moving. I felt utter respect and amazement.

For the past several miles I had mentally criticized his inefficient running form. He stood out in a crowd as a misfit. Now, as I watched him struggle with every step, I saw the determination in his eyes and jaw. I could feel the tears sliding down my cheeks knowing that this man, in all of his odd running form, was more of an athlete than I was. He had to make far greater effort to achieve the same result as me. He had every excuse to sit at home and avoid activities like this, but there he was, running side by side with me and so many others. I felt small for having judged him all those previous miles.

Since those experiences, I have tried to be slower to judge others. I had judged the gal in the Deseret News Marathon and the man from the New York Marathon both based on their physical attributes, and I was deeply humbled when I realized how wrong I was. Emotional and mental burdens are even more difficult to see, but are often heavier than physical limitations. I am learning to be more compassionate and empathetic. If people aren't kind to me, instead of internalizing their behavior I try to understand them. And, more often, if something doesn't negatively affect me directly, I have learned to respect the differences.

CHILD'S PLAY

"Keep smiling, because life is a beautiful thing and there's so much to smile about

—*Marilyn Monroe*

After school on Fridays, before we were free to enjoy our much-anticipated weekend of fun and relaxation, my mother schlepped my two sisters, brother, and me to piano lessons. I detested piano lessons. I hated every minute of them. I didn't find playing the piano a useful skill, an enjoyable activity, or a good use of my time—neither during the lessons nor the daily practicing that went along with them. If given the choice, I would have rather poked a thousand needles in my eye (I cross my heart!). My piano teacher was Mrs. Berger, whom we often called Mrs. Booger—hence my mother's subsequent demand that we call her only Mrs. B.

The single redeeming aspect of Friday night piano lessons was that beforehand my mom would take us out to eat fast food. This was a rare treat, mostly because of the limited options in our tiny town. To get to the fast food establishments we had to drive 20 minutes each way, which took the "fast" part out of it altogether. Except for Friday nights. Mrs. B. lived right next to Burger King and on lesson days we looked forward to those juicy burgers and crunchy fries. For a mere $2.22 one could get two burgers and two small fries, an irresistible deal. The food was so deliciously warm and salty we devoured it all.

Mrs. B. lived on a steep hill with a grassy slope. Mom would drop us off for two hours, leaving us to rotate through our 30-minute lessons. For the entire hour and a half it wasn't my turn with Mrs. B., I would chase my brother and sisters up the hill, lie down, and roll all the way to the bottom. With our arms crossed over our chests we raced. Often, someone's body would roll off course diagonally, and whomever that happened to would lose. Since each of us was stubborn and unwilling to walk away the loser, after every race someone would demand a rematch and we'd run back to the top of the hill, dizzily stumbling over our feet. Because I was allergic to grass I would pay for this fun for days afterward. My skin would itch and I'd break out in hives, my throat scratchy and my nose running. About the time I started feeling better it would be Friday night again, and the lure of the grassy hill would entice me with another chance of walking away the victor. In the wintertime, we opted to slide down the hill instead of roll.

Ideal childhoods are like that, riddled with endless hours for fun, imagination, and freedom. Kids think of racing downhill and warm, salty fries instead of allergies and dreaded piano lessons. As adults we tend to focus, instead, on all the work involved with anything. We think about climbing up the steep hill, rather than the wonderful flying feeling of high-speed rolling. We mature and we accept responsibility. And with this, a lot of us forget to have fun. We forget to let ourselves have joyful moments throughout the day. We stop looking for that fuzzy caterpillar on the sidewalk, taking the time to pick it up and let it tickle our skin as it crawls around our hand. We are too hurried to even notice the caterpillar.

When I became a runner, it allowed me to spend more time outside. My pace is slow enough that I can look around, enjoying the beauty of the outdoors and noticing the little details the way I used to. Once I started taking the time to enjoy the smallest of small blessings, life became exponentially more beautiful. The oranges, purples, and blues of the sunrise take my breath away. I notice the tiny buds that appear on the trees in springtime, which will slowly grow until the tree is full of big green leaves. Later in the year, autumn will change each of the leaves from green to orange, then red, then brown before they finally fall to the ground, where I'll feel the dried leaves crunch under my feet. I listen to the birds chirp in the trees as they welcome in the day. I see the overcast mornings when fog is like a blanket over the city. All of it is so beautiful. Why didn't I notice it before? It was there all along; I was just too busy to look.

Children roll down grassy hills, swing to feel the air blow through their hair, run through lawn sprinklers, always seeking fleeting moments of exhilaration. Like them I once again find myself filled with profound joy from the little things like I did during child's play. I relish those details, knowing that they will soon fade to memories.

And as I acknowledge these simple details, gratitude naturally flows. I slip my shoes on and run like a child. I try to reverse time and see the world the way I used to, amazed and bewildered at the stunning beauty of nature around me. I want to see, touch, and smell all of it, a child once again. I don't want to take any of it for granted. I resist the urge to let the stresses and burdens of adulthood distract me from life's simple pleasures. I want to feel free like a child, and when I run, I do.

DISCOURAGEMENT

"Even if you fall on your face, you're still moving forward."

—*Victor Kiam*

In college, I studied to be an accountant. Numbers have always come naturally to me and I loved how straightforward math problems were. Numbers are definitive; they remove ambiguity and disagreement. Accounting is like an advanced algebra class where assets minus liabilities equal owner's equity. The balance sheet, income statement, and cash flow intertwine and must balance. If there is an error, these reports won't agree with one another. When that happens one can easily find the discrepancy and make the necessary changes. The challenge is to ensure the accounting method employed is correct, but the details of the transactions are easy. I love numbers, financial statements, and working in the field of finance. The numbers tell the story about the health of the business. After analyzing the numbers, one can make the necessary decisions to adjust the business model and improve productivity.

The college accounting program was challenging, but not extraordinarily difficult. I took full loads of credits, attended college year-round, and was able to graduate with my bachelor's degree quickly. I took the GMAT, the entrance exam necessary to enroll in the MBA program, and enrolled in the Master of Science in Taxation program at the local university. I was also working as an accountant full time. Meanwhile, I decided to study for the CPA exam simultaneously with doing my master's program, while the information was fresh in my head.

The CPA exam was daunting. I had heard that on average it took seven times to pass. I took the CPA exam under rules established before the Uniform Accountancy Act changed the way the test is administered. When I took the exam, there were four parts to the test: audit, tax and governmental, financial, and business environment (business law). One could pass the test outright by passing each part with a score over 75%. One could "condition" the test by passing two of the parts with grades over 75% and passing the remaining two parts with scores over 50%. If the test were conditioned, the candidate would need only to retake the pieces with scores between 50-75%, making it much easier to pass the exam on future attempts.

My life was very full, but I didn't think sitting the CPA exam would be overly challenging if I did the work to get ready. I knew, though, that the exam was notoriously all-encompassing and difficult, with extremely detailed material where the slightest mistake would render an answer incorrect. I purchased review courses and studied hard for months. Although I was a bit daunted, I felt prepared. After the exam I thought I'd earned a passing score. I'd studied so diligently. The CPA exam is graded on a curve, so the results are not available until all the exams are graded; since part of the exam is written, this process takes quite a while. Under the old exam, it took two months.

Finally, I received a letter in the mail from the state board of accountancy. I was full of anxiety as I held the envelope in my hands. I had worked so hard, and my results were a reflection of all my previous years of schooling. I slowly opened the envelope and then the letter. I read the results. I had narrowly failed to pass the exam, causing me to also fail to condition the exam. I was distraught.

I had never experienced real failure before. My life experiences had taught me that if I worked hard and worked smart, I could accomplish anything I set my mind to. Academics were always easy for me, especially math and analytics. They had always come naturally and I found tasks like reconciling accounts soothing. Accounting was my safe place, my comfort zone. Failing after putting forth so much effort, not just in exam prep but in the prior years of accounting classes, was a bitter pill to swallow. It was humbling and infuriating all at once. I didn't know how I could have studied harder.

Self-doubt overcame me and I wondered if I had what it took to ever pass the exam. Had the last few years been a complete waste of time? My mind jumped to the worst. I imagined my inability to pass the CPA exam haunting me and my career, limiting job opportunities and promotions for years to come.

Then I dug in. The CPA exam, while arduous, was a summit I could reach. Many people did it each year. The questions had correct answers. With enough studying, I could learn enough to pass the exam. This was a doable task. If I tried hard enough, I would be a CPA. I had only failed by two points, a few questions. If I was willing to keep trying, this goal was within my reach. Once I made up my mind, I got back to work. It took a while, but eventually I passed.

Though I did persevere in the end, it was humbling. And through the pain I learned a lot about myself. I underestimated the difficulty of the test, and I also overestimated my ability to multitask. Academics had always come easily to me, but that didn't mean I couldn't fail in them, or in anything else in my life. Success eventually came, but failure came first.

The CPA exam is far from my only failure. I have applied for jobs I did not get, I struggled (and barely managed) to finish a 100-mile bike road race, and I have repeatedly failed to meet my goals in running. Although each of them hurt, I've learned that failing once (or several times) doesn't make you a failure. And the thing is, no one asks how many times I took the exam after learning that I am a CPA—it simply doesn't matter. What matters is that I did it. The day I read the letter from the American Institute of CPAs informing me that I had passed, it validated my belief that I am capable of anything I am willing to work for. It might not be easy and I might not succeed the first time, but that doesn't matter.

The more I've experienced failure, the better I've become at dealing with discouragement and gathering the courage to try again. To really try and give something your full effort leaves you in an emotional, vulnerable state where you're susceptible to rejection in its rawest form. Failure never loses its sting, but age and experience do help us develop the skills to move on more easily.

Running marathons has presented many opportunities to stretch myself well beyond my perceived abilities. Over the years as I've tried to break my personal best race times, discouragement has become familiar. In 2013, I signed up for the Rock 'n' Roll Marathon in Phoenix, Arizona. The January race date made for a difficult training season full of late fall and the snowly and often icy winter weather. On race day it felt good to see the sunshine. My joints were loose and happy in the Arizona heat. I hadn't planned on setting a PR when I trained, but I felt energetic and strong. When the race began I pushed a fast pace. Though I'd begun the race with no specific goal, that changed at the half marathon mark when I realized that if I could maintain pace, I would finish at around 3:15. My previous record was closer to 3:25. A 10-minute reduction in my overall time would be a huge improvement. I had just recovered from having my fourth baby and felt itchy to race hard. I wanted to prove to myself that even after kids, I was as good as I was before. Just like that, I had my mind set on a new personal record.

Full of excitement and with a newfound surge of energy, I went for it. I pushed hard. I could taste the victory in my mouth as the miles ticked by. My spur-of-the-moment goal was within my reach. I was doing it, one mile at a time. I imagined the phone call to my husband after the race where I'd proudly proclaim how wonderful it was and how well I'd done. I thought of the text message I would send to my running friends back home who had requested my finish time. Success was right around the corner!

And then things took a turn. At mile 18, my stomach started to hurt. For some reason my digestive tract was not absorbing the gel blocks I was eating, or the water and sports drinks I had been consuming. My stomach was cramping. I decided to pull back a little bit and shoot for a more realistic goal. I would be quite happy with a 3:20. That would still shave of a lot of time from my PR. I began bargaining with my body. Miles 19, 20, 21, and 22 slowly trudged by. The race was hard and getting harder. By mile 23, I had slowed to a stop. I wanted to lay down on the side of the road and wait to be dragged away by the sag wagon, the vehicle that drives the course offering rides to runners unable to finish. I'd gone from elated to broken—mentally, physically, and emotionally. I ran, jogged, and walked the remaining three miles to the finish line.

I ended up finishing with a respectable time, one I would have been perfectly content with ordinarily. It was a solid race and given my training conditions back in Washington, I should have been proud of myself. But I was more disappointed and discouraged than I had ever been before. I crossed the finish line, where my training partner was waiting for me. I ran right past her to a grassy area, put my head on my knees, and cried. I had prepared, trained through difficult conditions, and raced well—but I had failed to set a new PR. All that effort for nothing.

Sure, I finished the race, but I failed to meet my goal. Though it had been spontaneous, my goal represented something about who I was at my core: a runner, not simply a post-partum mom. Perhaps it was unrealistic to expect my body to perform better than it ever had before such a short time after giving birth. Maybe I wasn't taking into account my increasing age and decreasing energy levels when I fixed my mind on the PR. I also had a scary thought: would I ever be able to PR again? Perhaps my days as a contender for a fast marathon finish were in the past. This thought compounded my disappointment. The unknown nagged at me, making the sting of disappointment even more painful.

This, I've learned, is what happens when we dream big. I had finished marathons many times before. When I shifted my goal to finishing with a PR, I opened the potential for disappointment and discouragement. I put every ounce of effort I had on that racecourse and I failed. I pushed as hard as I could and had nothing to show for it. Instead of telling tales of glory and determination, I had to relay a sad story of defeat. It was not the story I prepared myself to tell. Moreover, it was not who I was. Quitter and failure aren't adjectives I use to describe myself, and these feelings agitated me.

Failure. Quitter. No, those aren't adjectives that describe me. Not when I failed the CPA exam, and not in running. I have learned that I love to fight through the despair of discouragement. What is that character trait that refuses to stop at failure? The one that gives you the determination to succeed, regardless of how many times you fail along the way? Certainly courage is an element, but for me it's primarily stubbornness. I am too stubborn to let failure be the final label attached to me. Thus far, I have been able to approach my goals with determination and a work ethic that eventually turn failure into success. While I failed several times after running the marathon in Arizona, years later I got the PR I was chasing. What I didn't know on that disappointing day was that my best race was years down the road with a PR that I couldn't have imagined in my wildest dreams. But I was only able to get there because I first overcame the discouragement of failing.

I will continue to set new goals, personally, professionally, and physically. I know that my body will eventually not be able to do what I am asking it to. I won't always see the improvement I yearn for. I will need to adjust my goals to my new capabilities. As I look forward into the future I am planning to start training for the Olympic Trials. My heart is timid because I have finally set a goal that I might not be able to achieve: it may not be physically possible for me to do this. But I understand myself well enough to know that, no matter what, I will try, and try, and try again.

CARPE DIEM

"What lies behind you and what lies in front of you, pales in comparison to what lies inside of you."

—*Ralph Waldo Emerson*

When I decided to run my first marathon, I had graduated college and was working at the corporate office for Albertson's in the accounting department. Our economy was quite sluggish and there was a sense of unease following the terrorist attacks on the Twin Towers. There were mandatory reductions in all the accounting departments and a lot of people were losing their jobs. For myself and other recent new hires, there were mandatory Saturday workdays and we were told that our new normal work hours were from 7:00 a.m. until 6:00 p.m.

We had an office walrus. He was actually a senior manager, but with his protruding chest, round chubby cheeks, and wickedly hairy mustache, a cartoon walrus was an obvious comparison. At 7:00 a.m. sharp, we would hear his office chair creak as he lifted his weight from it and tried to quietly maneuver out of his office. A man of that magnitude, though, cannot be sneaky. It was like an elephant trying to hide behind a tree. He would hold his hands behind his back and sneak around the office, tiptoeing quietly as he peered over the cubicle walls.

It was never communicated, but we knew what he was doing: silently taking attendance, noting those employees who were diligently working. If you made eye contact with the walrus, he would immediately avert his eyes, trying to appear casual—but being the bright cream-of-the-crop individuals we were, his true intent quickly became clear. We all knew he wasn't simply on his way to get his morning coffee; we were an office full of detail-oriented accountants. His routine and habits were obvious to us all.

This process was repeated at 7:30 sharp, only the walrus would walk around with a slight frown at the empty desks this time, making mental notes of who failed to show up for work. Again at 8:00 this process was repeated, except instead of a slight frown, his face puckered up tighter than a sphincter, his nose scrunched as if the nose hairs had been singed by rank flatulence. His face even turned a slight crimson color. You didn't want to make the mistake of having an empty chair on a regular basis for his second or third roll call.

In the economic environment of the turn of the century, the stock market was slow to recover and businesses were contracting, companies were laying off employees, and cost reductions were emphasized. The pressure and stress of the work environment increased as employees felt unsure about their future. Roll call was a way for management to differentiate the dedicated employees from those less interested in their jobs. In my company, should you find yourself on the absentee list during the third roll call, you were on the chopping block.

It was a lovely environment to work in. The stress was unbelievable. Aside from the attendance and the mandatory Saturday workdays, we all took pay cuts and there were routine employee eliminations. In efforts to make sure I wasn't ever one of the employees to get the axe, I worked even more. As long as the walrus saw my body in my chair more than the others, I knew I was safe. I got the smirk of approval instead of the laser-beam stare.

It was during this time that I thought it would be a good idea to get my master's degree. The corporation had a fairly good education reimbursement option and I needed some extra credits so I could qualify to sit for the CPA exam. It made sense to just get my master's as I earned those credits. I would work until 6:30 and grab some dinner on my way to my 7:00 class. These master's classes were held once a week from 7:00-10:00 p.m. I typically took two evening classes a semester. I thought about taking a lunch hour class or an earlier class, but I knew the walrus would disapprove. If I wanted to keep my employment and that coveted educational reimbursement, I had to work from early morning until evening.

Monday through Saturday were busy with work and school obligations. Perhaps I could throw a load of wash in while I was catching up with my studies. Because my husband and I both worked long hours, we were never home enough to make the house dirty and while our home was a decent size, most of the rooms never had anybody even go inside them. On rare occasions I found myself needing to go to the grocery store for food and supplies, but that was very sporadic.

In my master's program we were encouraged to "think outside the box." This was meant to urge us as future leaders in business to get creative about solving problems and approaching negotiations. Already slightly irritated because of the stressful work environment and my busy schedule, I stewed over this phrase. Something bothered me about it, yet I couldn't put my finger on what right away. The box. Me. I was inside the box. I needed to get out of the box to be successful. This message was repeated until I started to believe it. Until I thought for myself.

What box were they talking about, and why did they assume I was inside the box to begin with? I am only inside the box if I allow others to put me inside a box. I suppose conformity is the box, but I didn't feel like that described me. Moreover, this box felt claustrophobic and I wanted to make sure I was clearly outside of it. The corporate world was turning me into a robot, marching into work, sitting at my cube working at a computer, and then marching home. Work and my profession were putting an otherwise free spirit inside the box. A place I didn't want to be. A place that didn't feel comfortable.

I wanted to be free to be whoever and whatever I chose. I didn't want stereotypes attached to me based on my profession, gender, religion, education, socioeconomic status—nothing. I wanted to be independent of all those assumptions. I wanted to be myself, floating outside the box, doing what I loved. This stirring in my soul made me feel like a caged animal. I wanted out. I was in the box, and I needed to break free. I needed a release, an outlet.

This is why I began running. It gave me the feeling of freedom I had sought. The more I ran, the more I loved it. I ran more and more until I decided to enter a race. I was a busy woman and my schedule was tight, and I wondered if I should put off marathon training to a more convenient time. Maybe when the economy got better so I didn't have to work so much, or maybe when I found a different job. I would eventually graduate with my master's and get my evenings and weekends back. In the future things were bound to be better, right?

But, as we've all experienced, that didn't happen. Life just got busier. When I realized that, I decided that I was going to recycle "the box." It wasn't for me. I signed up for the marathon, even though I wasn't sure how I was going to fit training into my schedule. But I wanted to make sure I took opportunities to be the person I wanted to be, regardless of what others thought or expected. We get one chance in life to be happy. One chance to pursue dreams that are ours and ours alone to fulfill.

The office walrus helped me see who I didn't want to be. His approach to life, one tied so strictly to rules and protocol, is something I rejected. A life dictated by the clock, routine, and strict rules felt too controlled. He helped me see that I don't have to fit into other people's boxes to be successful. When I worked I realized I didn't want to be someone like him, and that helped me understand that my life doesn't need to make sense to anyone but myself. I realized that life has two paths: the safe route, driven by conformity, or the fun route, where I decide to follow my heart on whatever random tangents it leads to. Once I gave myself the freedom to be who I wanted, whatever that ended up meaning, that is when the fun began.

It is easy to get into the habit of thinking that someday in the future it will be simpler. It is easy to fall into the trap of living for the "when" instead of the "now." Luckily, I didn't wait for a less-hectic time that would never come. I decided to carpe diem. Now was as good a time as any. Life was busy and would always be busy. I am a busy person and if life didn't give me enough to do, I would go find something to do. That attitude has allowed me to follow my passions without wondering if I have time for them. I make time for what is important to me, and everything else just falls into place around it.

PAIN

"Pain is temporary. Pride is forever."

—Unknown

It is going to hurt. The pain I am about to endure is inevitable. There will be times when I want to quit. I try to trick myself into believing that because I have done this many times before I will have no trouble handling the pain, that I will once again push through the discomfort, but I know the truth. This time is different. This is the first time in 44 marathons where I am running for a specific finish time.

Tomorrow is the day I have been training for. The speed drills, the dietary changes, the years of accumulating knowledge and experience are all culminating with this race. As I think about the evolution of my running goals, I recall a time many years ago when my goal was simply to finish strong. Then, as my confidence grew, I tried to beat my personal best finish time. Now, here I am, trying to do something that was once unthinkable: run a marathon in under three hours.

Anxiety fills my body, so palpable I can almost taste it. It grows from the pit in my stomach and spreads to my fingertips and toes. A wave of nausea hits and for a minute, I think I am going to be sick. It will pass. I know this because the feeling has been coming and going for the last four days. I am extremely jittery and nervous. My body and my mind are preparing for what they know lies ahead.

I try to mentally prepare. I ask myself the obvious questions: Why? Why am I doing this? Why is it so important to push? Why is the status quo not enough? When will it be enough, if ever? Why am I inflicting pain upon myself?

The answer comes quickly: Growth. Without pain, I am unable to experience growth. Mentally, physically, emotionally, and spiritually. I cannot grow without the uncomfortable stretching and pushing that often hurts. Remaining stagnate is comfortable. But my safe zone is not where I will reach my peak potential.

My mind drifts to another time when the growth was painful. I remember how difficult that experience was— and how satisfied I felt once I had conquered it. The memories of that time are still fresh and raw, and as I think back I feel myself starting to prepare.

I was in my late twenties, a working professional and a mother of two. Telecommuting allowed me to work while my kids napped, but it robbed me of any spare time. Every minute of every day was scheduled and accounted for. My husband, Rich, had just been accepted to the University of

Pennsylvania's world class business school, Wharton. The program was an executive MBA, which allowed him to work a full-time job and fly to San Francisco on the weekends to attend all-day classes. Both of us, burdened with heavy responsibilities, were in survival mode.

I was also pregnant with my third child. I knew the first two years of the new baby's life—the length of my husband's MBA program—would be challenging. Essentially, I would be single parenting three children. After much debating about when the best time to attend the program would be, we had decided that him attending while the children were younger would be best. He would have his entire career to benefit from the knowledge he'd acquire, and the young kids would likely not remember his absence. Plus, I preferred not to tackle the teenage years alone!

And so we began the long days of endless work. Without the help that would have come if we'd had family living nearby, the care of the children and maintenance of the household fell squarely on my shoulders. It was a constant and heavy obligation that I tried to juggle with my career. Every day felt harder than the day before. My husband worked at his job until dinner time. We would eat as a family and then he'd retire for the evening to work on his MBA home study materials. As my belly grew and my energy waned, I felt pushed to my max. I was exhausted. A nearly 10-pound baby was weighing down my joints, bones, and muscles. Caring for a busy two-year-old and four-year-old absorbed any spare energy I had.

As I became physically exhausted, I felt my emotional and mental energy also decrease. Every day was long. I was overwhelmed, fighting to make it to a bedtime with my sanity intact. The baby came, giving my body a break from the constant physical weight, but in exchange I had a hungry newborn who wanted to nurse every 90 minutes, day and night. Without a solid span of sleep, I was now completely drained. My feet were heavy. Every movement was labored and lethargic.

Even through this time I kept running. Rather than taking more out of me, running gave me a temporary surge of energy, just enough of a boost to get through those days. I ran in the early mornings, craving the silence and the chance to center myself and prepare for each busy day. This time of solitude charged my batteries and gave me direction for the day's activities.

I knew there was no other way to deal with this challenge than to face it head on. My husband was not able to reduce his work or school load. Both obligations required full-time status. I knew that if I didn't take care of the needs of the family and home, more would be added to my husband's load and he wouldn't succeed in school, and then all of this would have been for nothing. I wanted to be a supportive wife and allow him to be successful. I knew that our family's future opportunities depended on his success. We'd started down this road, and now the most efficient way out was to continue right down the middle, pushing straight through to the end.

I muscled my way through this challenging time. I focused on some wise words from my aunt, who encouraged me to look for the positives instead of the negatives. This was not easy. However, I knew that I would push away my support system of friends and neighbors if all I did was complain in their presence. And so I harnessed my stubborn streak and made a decision to make the best out of this difficult endeavor. Stubbornness, a family character trait, can be a negative, but it has paid off whenever I have set my eye on a goal that seems out of reach. While I distracted myself by having fun with friends, I tried not to shift my burden to them. The one person I felt like I could let my walls down with was my grandma, Meize. She had been through hard experiences in her own life and always had wise words of encouragement. While she rarely sympathized, she always knew what to say to make me feel better, taking a genuine interest in my life and showing unconditional love. She seemed to understand what I was saying without me needing to actually spell everything out. Meize shared stories from her own life, which inspired me to be a better person. I wanted to be a strong woman like my grandmother.

Fatigue. Exhaustion. Defeat. Courage. Persistence. And finally victory. When graduation day came, I sat in Pennsylvania, surrounded by my then 18-month-old, four-year-old, and six-year-old. I caught myself staring at them. A benefit to having immersed myself in motherhood as their main care provider was that we formed a bond so tight that it will endure for years to come. We learned how to still have fun when life gets hard. I didn't succeed—we succeeded. We were all victorious. Rich graduated at the top of his class and earned some job promotions because of his new skillset. I was proud of Rich for following his dreams and for his achievements. I felt satisfied with the role I'd played in his success, knowing that he couldn't have done it without me. I felt optimistic that the future was going to be easier, with more opportunities for our family, and this hope made it all worth it.

I was proud of myself. I had dug deep and somehow found the strength to keep going, even when I didn't think I could. I had refused to let myself give in to negative thoughts of defeat. The unrelenting grind of giving until I could not give any more had taught me that I am capable of much more than I think. I learned that I am strong and independent. I can multitask and I am extremely organized because I had to fine-tune those skills. I had not only survived this experience, but by the end I had thrived.

The bagpipes began to play as the graduates slowly marched into the auditorium. After the pomp and circumstance and the speeches it was time for the graduates to walk across the stage to collect their diplomas. As my husband's name was called, I felt a tear slip down my cheek, followed by many more falling even quicker. I cried, not tears of joy that this experience was over, but for all the hard situations along the way where I'd had to be strong. I was tired of being strong. I cried now because I didn't let myself cry then. I cried not because he had graduated, but because I had made it!

And now, marathon morning is here. Runners are buzzing around, finding their proper corral. I feel calm, but I know the storm is about to come. As I inch up to the starting line I know it is now or never. I am about to work harder than I have ever worked in a race before.

The starting horn goes off and I tuck into the pace group for the three-hour marathon. Pace groups are one of the big benefits of larger races. They do the math for you. I know that if I can stick with these guys, I will be fine. But the pace is difficult for me. I mentally tick off the miles as they pass, calculating how much I have left to go. At mile six, I am just under a fourth of the way there. At mile eight, I am almost a third of the way done. At the 13-mile mark, I am halfway done, but I am exhausted. The 3:00 pace group has gone ahead, but the 3:05 pace group has not caught me yet. While I feel my sub-3:00 marathon goal slowly slipping out of reach, I know that it's not entirely too late to meet my goal. Will I be able to run the second half as fast as the first? Perhaps I can still run fast enough. This hope gives me the motivation I need to keep pushing. The unknown lies ahead and with curiosity, I run faster.

I see a girl with auburn hair and a green shirt just in front of me. To her side is a cyclist who is accompanying her to the finish line. She is in third place for the top females. I slide past her and the escort informs me that he will now be with me throughout the rest of my race should I stay in the top three spots. This turns out to be a stroke of luck and also a curse. I now have to pay attention to my pace, and also my place within the race. The bike at my side is a constant reminder of my position. If I slow down, the cyclist will drop me. As I run, I try to keep pace with the bike, struggling to maintain my overall place. But the bike also brings extra encouragement. As I encounter crowds sporadically sprinkled along the racecourse, he tells them that I am third and the spectators go wild. I feed off their energy, feeling adrenaline each time I hear the cheers. What motivates me the most is seeing the little girls. At the front of the pack, I am running mostly with men. I want the girls watching to see that they, too, can run with the boys. They can pass the boys!

Every step, every mile, I find myself digging deep. You can do this! I know you can, I think. I look at my arm. Earlier that morning before the race, I took a Sharpie and wrote, "She thought she could, and so she did" to remind myself that I am capable of anything and everything I set my mind to. As I glance at my reminder, now smeared across my skin, I feel inspired to keep going strong.

My body always gets the most tired between miles 18 and 23, and today is no exception. I am fatigued. My muscles are tightening and I can feel them throughout my body as I push them past the point of exhaustion. My left calf muscle is cramping, my hips are tight, and my eyes are tired. I am not sure I can hold my pace, and this thought is discouraging. As I walk through the aid stations to grab hydration, my body doesn't want to start running again. Just let me rest and walk a little longer! it cries. But my mind knows that unless I keep pushing, all of the hard work leading up to this point will have been for nothing.

As I race, I remember those long days with my babies while my husband was in MBA school and know I can dig deeper. Let's go, you can do this, I tell myself. You are not a quitter! You can do hard things, tough things. Even when you think you can't give any more, you can. I have seen you do it before and you can do it again. Stop thinking about how hard this is and just do it! Physical, emotional, and mental pain, you've done it before. My mind tells my legs to pick up and go. They obey.

Mile after mile, the battle rages between my head and my body. They argue and barter. If you run to the next aid station, I will let you walk through while drinking. Or, I'll let you walk this hill, but you need to run when you get to the top. I glance behind me to see if the girl in the green shirt has caught up. She is nowhere in sight, so I am able to relax and focus on these last few miles. Mile 23, mile 24, and mile 25 slowly tick by. I am now in my final mile.

Two songs on my iPhone. I just need to run through two more songs, and then I'll be done. Two younger men in white shirts slide in beside me. I just need to stay with them, draft off them, and listen to my two songs and I will be there, I tell myself. I can do this, I know I can. The end is in sight. I see the finish line and out of nowhere I get a burst of energy. I feel the kick and I power through it, my feet bounding across the metal pads. I collapse into a wheelchair. I finish as the third overall female racer in a marathon with over 25,000 participants. My feet are throbbing. A blister has formed on the pad of my right foot and under my left toenail. My legs are burning, stinging, from pushing my muscles to exhaustion.

My finish time is 3:07. The crowd is cheering ecstatically: they have just seen a third place runner cross the finish line! Their shouts of encouragement and excitement fall on deaf ears. I should be happy, but I am devastated.

I bend over to take off my shoes, socks, and compression socks. The tears start sneaking down my cheeks. I made it to the finish line. I feel a surge of mixed emotions rush through my body. I am thrilled that I ran a good marathon, racecourse and conditions considering. I am proud of my effort, but I am deeply discouraged after falling short of my goal.

As a veteran marathoner I have experienced this before. And I have learned from those experiences. It is okay to make space in my heart for all of these feelings to cohabitate. I can feel proud of my achievements while also being disappointed. Being disappointed in the inability to meet my personal goal doesn't have to detract from enjoying what I did achieve. After running 45 previous marathons, I now have the perspective and maturity to understand these mixed emotions. And more importantly, I understand that I have to give myself space for all these feelings to dwell in my heart until my head can process them.

While I didn't meet my goal, a sub-3:00 marathon will happen another day. I know it will, because I am not afraid of fear and pain. I am not afraid of hard work. I might fail the first time I try to reach a hard goal, but that failure won't stop me from trying and succeeding another time. I am too stubborn for that. I know the satisfaction I will feel once again, in marathons and in life, when I gather courage, face the pain, and persevere. And I know myself better than anyone. I know I can do it.

DISTRACTIONS

"To give anything less than your best is to sacrifice the gift."

—*Steve Prefontaine*

Hats off to the hardcore runners. The ones who would rather run through the water stops while having Gatorade splash all over their faces, necks, and chests than add a couple of seconds to their finish times. I salute those of you who are so obsessive with your training schedules and nutrition plans that you dare not deviate by eating even one extra French fry with dinner. Your dedication inspires me. To the woman in the Nike San Francisco marathon who chose to skip the portable outhouse and instead run the final six miles in soiled spandex (and walk around the finishers area and enjoy the ride home in them) instead of taking a few minutes to find a proper place, your dedication far surpasses mine. For those runners who would rather obsess about how heavy their running shoes are than simply increase their speed the old-fashioned way on the track, I applaud your willingness to throw money into our sport to gain that competitive edge.

Comparatively, I am a lazy runner, a hack. I have (gasp) never had a training log. I buy whatever shoes are on clearance on the discount websites. I don't stretch before or after my runs. Goodness, I don't even follow an official training plan. I never eat breakfast before a marathon and never take the recommended hydration while on the course. I have always marched to the beat of my own drum, wanting to explore and make my own decisions using my own analysis. Perhaps this is because I wasn't trained to be a runner. I didn't have a coach in my youth telling me what I should and shouldn't do; I figured it out in the quiet mornings all on my own, using the trial and error method. I didn't even know products existed to aid runners until I saw them showcased at race expos, or noticed them in magazines and on other runners. Ignorance kept running easy for me initially.

Running is a raw form of exercise. It's instinctive. If you have ever spent time with kids, you may have noticed that they run everywhere. When I go to a store with my kids and ask them to grab a bunch of bananas, they will literally run the 50 feet to the banana display and back. On the occasions at home when they need to go back to their rooms to turn the lights off, they run. They run spontaneously, simply because it's fun.

The simplicity of the sport is what calls to my heart. Life is complicated. Our schedules are so busy. Why would my recreation time, my relaxation time, my alone time need to be bogged down with the stress that comes with tracking every detail? I had grown to love simply slipping on my shoes and just letting my feet go. I liked that running was a time when I was free from stress and a rigid schedule. I liked how relaxed I felt when I ran and I didn't want to ruin that feeling with the stress of analyzing numbers. After successfully finishing my first marathon, though, I wondered if all the extra paraphernalia was worth the money and hassle. I was curious. Was I missing out?

And so for a time, I tried to be a runner like my other dedicated friends. We all had new Garmin watches that would tell us everything, including how bad our morning breath was on a scale of 1-10. We'd strap our iPhones to our bodies and wrap wires around ourselves so we could enjoy the latest mix on Pandora. Our waists were cluttered with athletes' belts, each containing no fewer than six small jars of hydration (separated into perfect serving sizes so we wouldn't even need to decide how much to drink), little loops to tuck GU packets into, Mace holders, and a general pocket for our IDs, credit cards, and lip balms. With our arms, waists, and wrists sporting all of these necessities, we were safe to venture out.

Previously, my routine before a run had always been to get up exactly 15 minutes before I needed to be somewhere. This allowed me to hit the snooze button exactly once, leaving roughly seven minutes to get out the door.

I then had to quietly drag myself to the bathroom and try to remember how to dress myself before my brain had adequately woken up. I am a lazy person, and when I had to gather all those things to pack along on a morning run—the watch, the GU, the belt, the Mace—I had to get up at least 30 minutes earlier. Not worth it. Soon afterward I quit packing all my gadgets and gizmos made in China. The only things I remember to bring each morning are my bedhead and morning breath. I am unwilling to even get up two minutes earlier to brush my teeth. I do a courtesy mouth rinse, but only because I can manage that while I'm throwing on my clothes.

The most interesting thing happened when I ditched my running technology: I became faster. I hit my all-time PR. Instead of being a slave to my running watch, constantly checking my current pace, overall pace, and overall time while calculating how much time I had left to my goal finish time, and then trying to mentally do the math to back into the pace I needed to adjust to in order to hit that mark—I ran with my heart. If I got tired, I slowed down. If I felt great, I pushed harder. I didn't need to remind myself every half a mile to check my pace and go through the math to see if I was on target. I just ran.

Not only did I run faster, I enjoyed it more. I thought technology might make me a better runner, but it just took the carefree simplicity out of the sport. It wasn't until I shed all that stuff that I felt my mind and my body make a connection. And then, only then, did I reach my true potential as a runner. I've tried to extrapolate that into the rest of my life. My family has as much or more technology as anyone else. My car has a DVD player, we all have our personal devices, a television on each floor, and various tools to make our life easier. Two of my children learned their ABCs, numbers, and basic reading from these tools.

However wonderful and useful they can be, though, it is equally important to unplug and live your life with your mind and your heart. To have quiet time to process your world and live with a purpose. In moderation, all of these tools can be wonderful sources of information. Used too much, they are distractions, and can prevent us from reaching our highest potential. Now I like to look at my life under a microscope and ask: What is distracting me from being my best? What should I get rid of to live better? What obligations should I drop? Who and what am I letting influence me? Ultimately, am I better with or without [fill in the blank] in my life?

Allowing myself to detach and clear the mind, to feel with the heart, has helped me enjoy the moment. Rather than obsessing over details, I find myself looking more at the big picture. As I run marathons, I can rarely remember a lot of specifics. I don't remember the course very often and usually won't recall the topography unless it is drastic. I detach, for the most part, and run with my heart. When I do this, I feel that freeing and liberating feeling I had when I started running. I fall in love with running all over again, just a girl in her shoes going on an adventure. And when I detach from life's distractions, obligations, electronics, and even people at times, I feel the same way. I'm just a girl on an adventure, falling in love with being alive.

HILLS

*"She was unstoppable not because she did not
have failures or doubts, but because she continued
despite them."*

—*Beau Taplin*

I have always lived in the Pacific Northwest, in Utah, Idaho, and Washington. The grand, bold, and beautiful Rocky Mountains were the backdrop of my childhood. In college I would hike them on the weekends, and in the winter my family and friends would ski the mountains. The rolling hills and altitude were just part of the terrain. Many professional runners will train in the high-altitude mountains of Colorado. The elevation of the Northwest teaches their bodies to perform on less oxygen, giving a competitive advantage when they race at lower altitudes or flatter terrain. I'm nowhere comparable to the elite athletes, but I have had my fair share of experience running in the mountains.

In January of 2013, I found myself in Phoenix for a race and as I was talking with a local about the racecourse, he kept referring to running up the mountain as the biggest challenge. I scanned my surroundings and was left utterly puzzled. He kept pointing to a mountain, but I couldn't see what he was talking about. I wondered if something was obstructing my view. I wanted to be mentally prepared, and if I was going to face a major hill, I wanted to know in which mile I could expect it. He kept pointing and seemed to be losing patience until I finally realized that the tiny hill in front of me was the mountain he was referring to.

I have spent the majority of the last decade living in the cute, resort-like town of Liberty Lake, Washington. I love the evergreen mountains surrounding my home; they are stunningly beautiful, especially in the winter. The branches hold snow on the pine needles so delicately. My husband and I built a house on the top of one of these mountains, a mile and a half straight up the hill. On the backside of the mountain, the road meanders up a slope along the lakeside view. While the front of the mountain is a grueling mile and a half climb, the backside is two and a half miles of rolling hills.

Once a week, a group of running friends and I gather to run the hill. We run it three times, up the front side and down the backside. In just over an hour and a half, you can run a heart-pounding three-loop repeat. On the third round of hills, my heart will beat so hard it feels like it will burst out of my chest. As I huff and puff up the hill, the cool air stinging my lungs, I feel every muscle movement as if in slow motion. I have a love-hate relationship with this hill.

Hills are a hard workout and will leave you sore for days; very few workouts will give you that burning sensation more quickly. But the lactic acid eventually goes away and the soreness fades, and before long you realize that you are stronger. Hills are essential to maintaining fitness and can be used for growth. When you used to slow down or take walk breaks, now you can keep powering up to the top. Before long, they aren't scary anymore. They become old friends you've made peace with, sharing a silent agreement: I promise to see you often and embrace you, and you promise to make me work hard.

In 2015 I decided last minute to run a local marathon in Coeur d'Alene, Idaho. It is a fantastic race only 15 minutes away from our home in the panhandle of Idaho. The race starts at the park to the side of a resort. The first few miles twist and turn through the surrounding neighborhoods. Then, runners are channeled onto a pedestrian path with the lake on the right-hand side and mountains to the left. It is peaceful and serene, with the thick evergreens giving off a delicious forest smell. Around mile seven, nestled in the middle of the route is a long and steep hill. The hill is almost a mile long with a steady incline. The back of the hill is half as long and twice as steep. Running up the hill requires a lot of effort; it seems to stretch on endlessly.

The decline of the hill is barely noticeable when recovering from the challenging climb. Because it is an out-and-back course, runners are faced with the challenge twice.

The CdA race is held at the end of May. I had just run the Kentucky Derby Festival Marathon in April, where I set a new personal record of 3:21. For this race, my expectations were low—all I wanted was an enjoyable run in my hometown. That year, I ran a total of 10 marathons, with this one coming mid-year. Not all of them counted toward my 50 state marathon goal, including this one (I'd already run an Idaho marathon in 2009). For this race, I simply wanted to enjoy the experience and finish strong. Sleeping in my own bed and not having to travel for the marathon helped take away the pressure I normally feel, and the days leading up to it were relaxing and peaceful as opposed to hectic with travel scheduling, time changes, and the logistics of a new city.

Just a few months previously, my husband had decided to start looking for another job. I knew a job change would likely take us away from the beautiful area I had grown to love. As I ran the course in the place I've grown to love, my heart was full of gratitude. I thought about all my babies born in the area and all the memories we had created. I had first moved away from our extended family to eastern Washington, just west of the Idaho border, as a brand-new mom at the young age of 25, then an employed professional and inexperienced in life. So much had changed since then. I was mentally preparing to leave as a transformed person.

As I faced those hills on the CdA marathon course I had an epiphany. Life is a series of hills. We might feel scared and unsure of our ability when faced with a new challenge, but the only way to get to the top is one step at a time, regardless how small each step might be.

When I came to Washington, I was still trying to figure out who I was and what I wanted out of life. Through personal discovery, much of it gained through running, I will be leaving a more confident and driven person. This knowledge will become a foundation for me to reflect upon in the future when I struggle with uncomfortable change. As I ran the CdA marathon, I pondered the difficult experiences I'd had over my years in the area. I had moved away from family and friends, and it had been very difficult not having their regular presence in my life. I'd felt scared and unsure, often as though I had no other choice but to stand tall and press on. Life was tough. It was scary. There was only one way to move past this challenge and that was to start taking steps forward. Sometimes those steps had a nice long stride and sometimes they were baby steps. Each step was what I could do at the time. I couldn't demand more of myself than I was able to give, a lesson I would later apply to my personal life.

Oftentimes we will see a challenge in life and shy away from trying to climb the hill. We think of all the reasons why we can't do something. It is going to be hard! I don't have the energy! What if I fail and end up walking the whole way? But if we want the rewards and the self-satisfaction of enjoying the view at the top of the climb, there is only one way. Lacing up those shoes and taking one step after another. One of my favorite sayings is "How do you eat an elephant? One bite at a time." And so it is with hills and every other challenge in life. One step at a time. One day at a time. It is conquering those difficult tasks that creates confidence that you can tackle the next challenge that comes your way. Hills shouldn't be feared, but rather welcomed as opportunities for growth.

Hills, those grueling challenges. Hills can be beasts and they can get inside your head. Sometimes your worst enemy is the voice in our head that plants those seeds of doubt. Having overcome challenges in the past helps me quiet those negative thoughts and gives me the confidence to know that I can conquer what I am faced with. And with each success, I have more in my arsenal to draw from when faced with my next challenge. The voices can make you question your abilities. They can be discouraging. They can even convince you that you can't and make you stop in your tracks. Once you tackle those demons in your head and stop letting them tell you that you can't, you'll realize that you can.

Our life challenges will help us develop a unique set of skills, including perseverance and determination, to be able to deal with the next challenge we are given. And after the challenge is over the reward is self-confidence. The sooner we can look at a challenge, like a hill, and view it as a learning process that will make us a better person, the easier it is to accept the challenge.

When I first decided to run a marathon in all 50 states, I knew it would be hard. I knew that every race wouldn't be under ideal situations. I knew that a goal that big would take a lot of dedication. I knew that life would ebb and flow, but that somehow, I would need to stay committed to my goal. As it is with running, so it is with life. If my husband accepts a new job in some other city, I will pack my family up, sell my home, purchase a new home and move away from the friends who have become my family. I will stand at the bottom of that hill and one step at a time, I will move toward the summit.

SCARF

"If we couldn't laugh, we would all go insane."

—*Robert Frost*

I suffer from MUMOA (Making Up My Own Acronyms) and PMGDE (Post Marathon Garbage Disposal Eating). Marathoning has brought new awareness into my life, and through it I've become acutely cognizant of the many phases of my own eating.

After a race, I will immediately enter Phase One, which I lovingly refer to as the "barf" phase. Usually during a marathon I will experience indigestion or gastrointestinal discomfort where my stomach cramps so much that food seems like a punishment. Water is the best remedy for this ailment, unless a cold Diet Coke is on hand. Diet Coke is the cure-all in Tami Town, and the RX is as much quantity as possible. Whatever the ailment, the first step to recovery is a Diet Coke. This thirst-quenching, headache-removing, bubbly cold beverage can often be spotted lovingly coddled by my left hand. Nicknamed my "tall, dark, and handsome," I open my arms to the first love of my life to comfort and soothe me. Even while suffering from the "barf" feeling, I can always find a way to choke down a Diet Coke. Never in my life have the words "I just don't feel like one" ever passed my lips.

Should I feel well enough to consume solid food, I will enter Phase Two: the "scarf" phase, otherwise known as the "garbage disposal" phase. While Phase One can last anywhere between two and 24 hours after the race, Phase Two is bound to last much longer, a minimum of 24 hours and up to 48 hours. During Phase Two, I attempt to eat anything that isn't nailed down, including but not limited to the barstool or family cat. During Phase 2 I will eat anything and everything, never getting that satisfied feeling. If you can dip it in BBQ sauce or ranch, it's considered edible. It is imperative that I don't find myself in any social situations during Phase Two. Humiliation will occur after the shock of the onlookers is observed. It is also important that as much healthy food as possible be available for consumption, as well as endless carbs. If I can manage to eat mostly healthy food now, I won't feel as ashamed and embarrassed once I've moved through each phase of post-marathon eating and returned to normalcy. Unfortunately, as much as I try to eat healthy, it's the unhealthy food my body craves. The hidden bags of Peanut M&M's are found, no-bake cookies are made and simultaneously consumed, and ice cream is eaten straight out of the carton.

During Phase Two, I cannot go to Costco. If I do, the sweet aroma of bite-sized snacks beckons and I circle the sample tables, feeding my insatiable appetite. And, I purchase everything. Should the coupon book overflow with great deals, I find myself buying multiples of items I shouldn't have even bought one of. Who really needs four bags of Peanut M&M's? No one! However, when they are delicious and $3.50 off of the regular price, I grab the maximum number allowed. As you can imagine, it is very important that my pantry not contain snack foods, candy, chips, or easily-prepared food during Phase 2. I count on my hatred of cooking to deter my consumption. As hungry as I get, there are foods I still can't choke down, like ramen and hot dogs. These horribly processed food items—the only things I can pass up—are what my kids will eat until I exit Phase Two. Once I have regained control of myself, I can resume cooking edible food.

Phase Three, the "ostrich" phase, occurs as I realize the effects of Phase Two. Binging on sugar will have left my throat raw—and it was already experiencing a burning sensation from the endless flow of Diet Coke. The guilt! The shame! I'll slink past the bathroom scale, knowing that despite the calories burned during my marathon, I've gained weight during Phase Two. Phase Three is all about regaining balance. But honestly, it's also about trying to ignore and forget Phase Two by acting like an ostrich and sticking my head in the sand.

In Phase Three I try to drink more water, eat fruits and veggies, and shun my beloved sweets. It's a mental game of sorts. The voices in my head attempt to coax me into continuing Phase Two. I've earned it, they will say. Just a little bit more! On occasion the voices will persuade my right arm to betray me. If I allow the right arm to reach into that bowl of M&M's, I know the battle is lost. I tell myself I'll only have a small handful of eight to 10 of those chocolaty, candy-coated treats. It isn't until I'm scratching the bottom of the bowl that I realize I've relapsed into Phase Two. A relapse into Phase Two will eventually push me back into Phase Three. And the voices in my head will quiet down enough that I'll finally find the balance in my diet I'm looking for. At least for a few days, until another long run or marathon occurs. It's a never-ending cycle.

I use humor to mask topics I prefer to avoid. By using jokes I distract others and often myself. However, nutrition hasn't always been something I approached with humor. There was a time in my life where it was a very serious matter, and it is something I struggle with.

Just recently, I hired a nutritionist. After two decades of disordered eating in different variations, I decided that it was time to seek help. Even with that help, it hasn't been an easy process. I believe in transparency, honesty, and vulnerability, and that's why I want to share this piece of my life. While revealing this part of myself is painful and even embarrassing, it is more important to me to be genuine. And so as Paul Harvey says, here's "the rest of the story..."

DEMONS

*"Believe in yourself and all that you are. Know that
there is something inside you that is greater than
any obstacle."*

—*Christian D. Larson*

My relationship with food hasn't always been something
to laugh about. I have struggled with food for decades.
In high school, I lost a lot of weight because of restrictive
eating. Initially it wasn't intentional. I remember the first
time I realized I had unknowingly gone a whole day without eating. I was lying in bed and my stomach hurt from
hunger pains. I couldn't remember what I had eaten that
day. Then it dawned on me that I hadn't had anything. It
was typical for me to skip breakfast, and lunch was hit and
miss depending on what was served in the cafeteria that

day and if I was too busy socializing to focus on food. With busy after-school activities, the day had just gotten away from me.

The sting of the acid in my stomach felt strangely good. I felt an odd sense of control knowing that my mind was stronger than my body. As that realization set in, I felt euphoric. The power I had over my body felt better than eating. I liked that feeling. In fact, I loved it. Knowing I was mentally tough gave me a sense of pride and accomplishment. Most people struggled to limit their food intake, but I was so mentally in control that I didn't even need to eat at all. It was a power rush and I quickly became addicted to that high.

Having control over my food was the only benefit I derived from this habit. There were many more detrimental side effects. Of course, I lost a lot of weight. That wasn't my intent or desired outcome, but I suppose it didn't bother me either. When my hair started falling out and my fingernails became brittle, I was finally forced to take notice of the negative physical side effects. I was cold all the time because I had extremely low body fat. I started wearing layers of clothing, not only to keep warm but also to stop people from staring at the sharp angles of my body. My immune system was weak. I got sick more frequently and didn't recover as quickly. What bothered me the most was my lack of focus. Academics were extremely important to me, and I had a harder and harder time staying alert.

I was stuck in limbo, wanting to have control and getting that sensation through limiting my food intake while not wanting the negative side effects of my choice. My body also felt that same physical strife. It was hungry and wanted nourishment. My mind didn't want to give it permission to eat. It was a constant battle. I was always exhausted. In all, my distorted relationship with food lasted years. I struggled for most of high school with what was "good" and "bad" food. If I deemed a food "good," I allowed myself to have it. If not, I would reject it entirely. There was no moderation, and there was no logical reason for how I differentiated between the good and bad foods. Mostly, I chose not to eat foods with high fat content (thinking that eating fat would make me fat) like meat and cheese. I preferred foods with high carbohydrates like breads, cereals, and sugar candy. I was lost and confused. I liked the positive affirmation I kept getting based on how I looked, but I felt terrible. Looking back I think of myself like Alice in Wonderland, traveling through shrinking hallways, with confusing messages floating through my head.

My parents considered checking me into an inpatient facility where I could receive professional help. I felt guilty watching the anguish I was putting them through, but even in the midst of that I felt self-satisfaction at my sense of control. I was transitioning from child to adult and the end of high school was approaching. While I was successful in academics and had a healthy social life, my world felt so busy and dynamic and I needed something I could control, anything! I knew my actions were hurtful, but they also felt good. I knew I was unhealthy, but I thought I looked good. It was all really confusing when I tried to think about it, so I chose not to. I latched on to this eating disorder as a core part of who I was.

I didn't end up going to an inpatient facility. When weighing out the benefits and drawbacks, my parents decided I was better off at home, in school and where we could still be together as a family. We worked through this issue with love, support, and education. As I learned about proper nutrition, I was able to understand that I needed to feed my body. Before my eating disorder I didn't know what a calorie was. That calories could come in the form of protein, carbohydrates, or fats wasn't part of my awareness. I didn't know my basic needs to survive, let alone to feed my body as it grew. As we educated ourselves, I slowly pulled myself out of suppressed eating. This process, in all, took about two years. I would make progress, have regressions, learn, and continue to try harder. And eventually, my mind stopped feeling the constant need for control over my body.

But while I had stopped starving my body, I still had a skewed relationship with food. College was a fresh start, where no one knew my past and I could turn the page to a new chapter in my life. While I no longer had a restrictive eating disorder, I did have a twisted relationship that continued for many years. I wonder if it will ever really be extinct. I still see remnants of my distorted view on nutrition slide in and out of my life.

I continue to believe certain foods are "good" and "bad," and often these categories have no basis in fact. But because my eating patterns can be passed off as simply picky or particular, I fit on the bell curve of normal eating. However, because my picky eating has its roots in my eating disorder, I see these as traces to my past. They are reminders that while I have made a lot of progress, I still have tendencies that I need to monitor.

During high school while I was learning about weight gain and loss, the analytical side of my personality liked learning that weight is really a math equation. If calories in exceed calories out, there is weight gain. If calories out exceed calories in, then weight loss will occur. During college I began to exercise as a way to manage my weight on the other end of the equation. While I was no longer restricting my intake, I was watching my caloric burn. Socially, this was far more acceptable since I could go out on a date to dinner and attend parties and functions without drawing attention to my lack of eating. No one seemed to mind if I went for a run.

Because of the damage I did to my growing body in my teen years, I have never had a regular reproductive cycle, and I didn't realize I was pregnant until a couple of months into each of my pregnancies, when my pants started to feel tight. Then I would take a pregnancy test and it would confirm what I had suspected. Thanks to modern medicine, the fetus would be measured in an ultrasound and I would have a delivery date calculated for me. Pregnancy awoke my old demons. I had no control over the changes that were happening to my body! A little alien creature had invaded. It was like a parasite, leaching nutrients from my bones, leaving me tired all the time. I had to think about the food that I was eating because somebody else depended on those nutrients for critical growth. I couldn't drink as much Diet Coke, in case the chemicals could be harmful. The lack of caffeine made me even more tired. I was constantly hungry. While I normally didn't eat breakfast, I was now forced to feed myself something in the morning, for the sake of this growing little person. I love to sprawl out on my stomach when I sleep. This too came to an end. During pregnancy, I felt almost no control over my life. And with everything changing, permanently, with the addition of each new person to care for, I wanted control more than anything.

The one thing that I found extreme joy in, that I kept all for myself, was running. I continued to wake up in the early morning hours throughout each pregnancy. Even with running, though, there was a lot that was out of my control. As my belly grew larger and larger, running became more difficult because of my size, my changing center of gravity, and the pregnancy hormones. My limbs were not as able to take the additional pounding my pregnant body put them through.

I often didn't even recognize who I was becoming. When pregnant I did not feel like myself. I craved control the way I used to. I was tempted to find that control through what I ate. Every day I had to choose: did I want to feed my baby the nutrients it deserved, or did I want to feed my demons? Which did I love more? Which was a higher priority to me? I knew that if I didn't give my baby proper nutrition, it would affect his or her life, permanently.

It was a daily struggle to make the right choice. Becoming a mother is always a sacrifice, but this sense of sacrifice set in very early on, way before a baby was even born. It was the first of many sacrifices I would be making as a parent. I would have to learn to put somebody else above myself, and I would have to learn how to take care of myself so my body could take care of somebody else.

I did my best to avoid slipping into my old patterns. With each pregnancy I asked the doctor to only notify me if I had not gained the recommended amount of weight or if I was gaining too much, rather than telling me any exact numbers. I put my home scale away and refused to let myself track my weight gain. In each pregnancy the doctors told me that my baby was healthy and growing, and that was sufficient feedback.

My smallest baby was eight pounds, and my largest baby was just under 10 pounds. Each of my babies was born between one and three weeks early. If they were born full term, they would've been larger! I let my body gain the weight necessary to grow healthy human beings. Each time it was a victory, and while it might not seem like much of an accomplishment, the daily battles I fought and won are some of the things I am most proud of. My heart and my mind agreed that the health of my children was more important than my personal tendencies. While I felt out of control of my body during pregnancy, I felt in control of my demons.

At times even now I am tempted by them again. During a move, job changes, or stress, I know where I could regain a sense of control: through my eating. When my life seems like a twister, my eating disorder is the eye of the storm. Everything else appears calm when I am in control. This scares me because I know the eating disorder is a destructive monster that wears a pretty smile and appeals to my subconscious. Unfortunately, it is how my mind deals with stress, my go-to button when there is too much change. Even after years of fighting them off, my demons still say all the right things, hoping to get me to do what they want me to. Skip breakfast, limit your calories, exercise more, only eat this type of food, don't eat that because it's bad. I have heard it all before. I am tempted to be in control again, because it feels good. There is a certain power in knowing that you can stop something from happening, even when it's the most natural and primal activity. Even when your life depends on it. At times it's still a daily, hourly, sometimes every-minute fight against these demons.

But I recognize the demons now. I've looked them in the eye. We've waltzed, we have a long-term relationship, and we are in a constant battle with each other. I know how they speak to me. I know how they entice me. I realize that this will always be a struggle for me, and acknowledging the struggle actually gives me a different kind of power, a different kind of peace. Life isn't controllable but more of a beautiful mess, and I try to embrace that. Sometimes the demons are loud, screaming in my ear about all the different ways I can take control again. Other times, they whisper ever so softly. But as I learned in pregnancy, if

I'm going to be the type of mom I hope to be, the kind of person I want to be, I need to also be healthy and strong. I cannot give in to the voices in my head. If I have a healthy and strong body, I have to feed it. I realize now that I am important enough to take care of properly.

As I've developed as a runner, I've chosen not to make nutrition a major issue because I know it's not what is best for me. Instead of fixating on control issues, I choose to give myself permission after a race to indulge in foods that will replace and repair what needs it. I choose to let food be a natural reward for hard physical exertion. If I try to control how I feed my body, I know it is a slippery slope. What is best for my mind and body is to let it go entirely. By giving up control, I feel more in control. I eat to live my life. I don't live my life to eat. Food is strictly functional and I'm glad it's there.

We all have voices in our heads, our own personal demons that know our weaknesses. They know just how to tell us we're not good enough. Sometimes they encourage us to try the latest fad diet in hopes of a quick fix. At times they might suggest that it is a good idea to take high doses of supplements. They know how to convince us to do something that is not good for our spiritual, mental, emotional, and physical selves. It's hard to admit weaknesses—but when we acknowledge them, openly and without shame, them that's when we start to push our demons out.

I will never escape my demons entirely. They are always there. I can, however, choose to listen. I can choose to act. Or, I can choose to ignore. With time, experience, and perspective, I now see correlations and know the triggers. When backed into a corner, we often have to choose our demons or our loves ones. Drugs, alcohol, diets, gambling, spending—they all have their appeal, and they all require a price to be paid. The battle is so real. But continuing to win that battle is a badge of honor I proudly wear, just like the extra 15 pounds I've carried around since I stopped starving myself. Those pounds, like my slightly larger thighs, are proof that I won my personal battle. My shining medal of recognition is having a little junk in my trunk and the absence of a thigh gap. My reward for steadfast dedication to addressing my demons is four healthy children who outsmart, outwit, and keep me laughing with their ingenuity. I win.

NO REGRETS

"Lord, grant that I may always desire more than I can accomplish."

—Michelangelo

I looked at the sticky ExerSaucer sitting in the middle of my living room floor. Next to it were the jumper, the swing, and the high chair. In addition to the big equipment were hundreds of little toys we had accumulated over the last decade. Years of birthdays, Christmas celebrations, Easters, and other gifting opportunities had left my house filled to the brim with kid stuff. I felt claustrophobic looking at everything piled along the walls, in the closets, and stacked on the shelves. The toys and gadgets were taking over the house. After cleaning around and under all of it, I suddenly realized we didn't even use these things that much anymore. And then, in a moment of genius, I decided it was time to dispose of these items. I never wanted to see them again.

My four children were all born within a decade of each other, and I loved having so many little people in the house. Their laughter filled our home with love, and nothing made my heart swell more than watching my older children gush over a new baby in our family.

Because of their evenly-spaced births every couple of years, I never got a break from the baby gear. It became a permanent fixture in my house. Just as one was outgrowing a toy, the next child began to show interest. Now, though, even our fourth and final baby was getting bigger. (Although I love being my kids' mother, the idea of having another person inhabit my body is about appealing as eating toe jam.) I eyeballed the toys with a mixture of feelings. I recalled seeing each of my children chewing on them, playing with them, and finally outgrowing them. The toys had woven themselves into the memories of raising my babies. I could remember how each of them had been acquired—the birthday parties with friends and family, the Christmas celebrations and special events. The toys were the backdrop of happy moments of motherhood.

Some mothers get sentimental when tucking their darlings' toys away and even cry as old equipment leaves the home. Not me. Purging began slowly and cautiously as I started looking around at the things we hadn't used in a while. The baby swing hadn't been occupied for several weeks and the baby might be too big for it now anyway.

Since he was becoming mobile, he didn't like being in the ExerSausers, either. The bouncy chair had been a place to feed the baby when he was small, but now he sat in the high chair, so I also tossed that in the pile to give away. Before I knew it, I had accumulated a mountain of stuff to get rid of. Thanks to social media, I easily sent out a quick announcement listing all of the gear available for free on a first come, first served basis. By that evening it was all gone. After 10 years of clutter filling the house, it felt like I had taken a long, hot shower. So cleansing and refreshing!

Oh boy, it felt so good that I made time in my schedule the following week to continue the purge. I started with all the baby clothes and onesies I knew I would never need again. Gone. Burp cloths and bibs, adios! To the multitude of blankets and jammies I had been hording for those repetitive throw-ups, spit-ups, and diaper leaks, ciao! Not only did it feel good to watch them go out the door, I knew the families that were taking everything would enjoy and appreciate it like I had.

Now I was hooked, and I knew what I had to do next. I waited quietly and patiently until a few days later when my older children were in school and the smallest was taking a nap. Then I tiptoed around the house tackling each of our three toy rooms. Yes, we had three toy rooms. I have four children who have been spoiled by friends and family at every holiday for years. We had accumulated so many toys they spilled into nearly every room in our house. Imagine my delight as I purged so many toys that I was able to consolidate all of them into one room. To my horror, I found that we had seven car and track toys, three separate train systems, and enough stuffed animals to fill a house in a developing country. So many generous gifts had infiltrated my home and I needed to simplify. The excess was disgusting and it was making me feel trapped.

Grateful for the endurance I had built up over my running career, I ran up and down the stairs collecting toys and stuffing them into a garbage bag. Nothing was safe. I went through the drawers in my kids' rooms, a madwoman frantically digging and tossing. When a bag was full, I hustled down to stuff it into my SUV. Stairs, sprints, high knees, heavy lifting—motherhood is the ultimate cross-training. When I was done, I had nine trash bags full of toys.

My time was up. The children needed to be picked up from school and I had to wake up the baby from his afternoon nap. I knew if I didn't hide the bags before the kids got home, they would dig through them, remembering the toys they'd forgotten about ages ago, suddenly claiming each one was their favorite. But I knew these toys hadn't been played with for months, if not years. As long as they didn't see what I was doing, they would never even know what was gone. Getting rid of the bags before the kids got home from school was an urgent matter that required immediate attention.

I stuffed the last bag into my car, utilizing my drishti breaths. Finding your drishti is a technique I learned in yoga where you breathe in through the nose and out through the mouth. Drishti breaths calm the nervous system, help you center your heart, and clear your thoughts. These deep and intentional breaths helped me quickly sort through the emotions flooding my body—excitement, happiness, anxiousness. If I pulled off the great toy heist, it would open the door for even more purging. I felt my nervous system calming as I prepared the baby's milk and went to wake him from his slumber.

I don't know how victorious Napoleon felt as he rode through the streets of Paris and through the Arc de Triomphe, but my level of accomplishment seemed comparable. I, Tami, was superwoman. I quickly loaded the baby into his seat and drove to the nearest Goodwill on the way to school pick-up.

I wasn't especially sad about giving away my kids' childhood mementos. I would have expected to feel differently as I closed a door on a season of life, one I had loved. Surprisingly, this was not how I felt at all. For the most part I was happy and peaceful. I had to wonder: What did that mean?

I was still wondering when I went on my next long run, my favorite time to think, uninterrupted. How can one be happy and sad about the exact same thing? How can you look at an item with nothing but warm, fuzzy feelings, yet be happy to toss it at your earliest convenience? How can I look at my children's infancy and toddler stages and have nothing but love for my time spent with them, but be so excited that the stage is over? I was confused. Was I sad? Happy? Excited? Wistful? My feelings were as diverse as bag of Skittles.

Over the next few weeks, I invested miles of thought therapy into the subject. I finally concluded that for me, when a job is done right mixed feelings are normal. I loved (and still do) being a mom with little children. Their joy, playfulness, and love are freely given. Having small children taught me a lot about charity, compassion, empathy, and selfless service to others. I had learned how to put my needs and desires second to the happiness of my children. I absolutely loved every minute of it, but it exhausted me. I didn't miss a single moment of my babies growing up. I'm happy with how I spent my time with them. I chose to stay home when they were young, and that was the right decision for me. I wouldn't go back and do it again, because I did the best I could at the time. As much as I loved parenting babies and toddlers, I am able to move forward into the next phase of life without sadness and regret, without wondering about the ifs and the buts. I have come to the understanding that when I do my best, I feel peace in my heart. I can move on because I know the future holds more experiences that will give me more opportunities to develop.

How relevant this is to running a race. My marathon finish times vary greatly depending on so many factors. Did I have a strong training session? What was going on in my personal life? How was my nutrition? Did the race-course lend itself to a good time? How was the weather the day of the race? Did the travel to the race wipe me out? Each race has a different story and a different chain of events that led to the various conclusions. What I've learned is this: If I do my best—in running, in parent-hood, in anything that matters to me—I can confidently move forward without regrets, regardless of what my best was at the time. I might hit an all-time fastest marathon or I might have to walk for miles. Either way, if I know that I gave 100%, I won't beat myself up about what might have been.

THE VOICE

*"He who is not courageous enough to take risks
will accomplish nothing in life."*

—Muhammad Ali

Bing! I received a text message from one of my best friends. I just saw her minutes ago when we finished our morning run. During our runs, we talk about everything, as I do with my other running friends. Running gives us the time to listen to the long versions of stories, to hear the details that often get left out in the summary of a short conversation. Because we usually run eight to 10 miles on weekdays and 18-20 miles on the weekends, we typically don't text or talk on the phone much aside from short messages regarding where and when to meet for our next run. Yet, after being apart for only a few minutes, there are sometimes bits of unsaid conversation that need to be shared.

Bing! Bing! Bing! My phone was vibrating nonstop with new messages. The first phone call or text isn't alarming, but when my phone receives many messages quickly, I check to see if it's an emergency.

Her: You were fast today. I'm going to start calling you the Tower of Power!

Me: You were right there next to me girl, way to go.

Her: Sidebar, do you remember a couple of years ago when I said you weren't living up to your potential?

Me: Yes….

Her: Look at how much faster you've become just this year!

Me: It's because this is the first time I've been able to train more than a few years without taking a pregnancy break. My strength and fitness is improving.

Her: I'm putting a new challenge in front of you that I want you to think about.

Me: Oh no, I'm afraid to ask. What?

Her: I want you to qualify for the Olympic Trials. You can do this! With every part of my being, I know that you can.

Me: The qualifying time is 2:45. My fastest marathon is 3:17!

Her: I know. We can talk about what training plan you'll need to use tomorrow on our run. Think about it.

I put my phone down and laughed out loud. This text exchange was so like her. She believes in me and plants seeds of hope, ambition, and desire. And she is as persistent as hell. The next morning she greeted me with a smile and asked if I was ready to start training for the Olympic Trials. And when that was over she said we should sign up for an Ironman. "Don't worry," she assured me. "I've hired a coach and we are going to do this together."

I once lacked confidence in my running abilities. Words of encouragement were essential to my psyche as I set out to run the marathon distance. As I gained confidence, I started seeing my prior self in others, runners toeing the line for the first time. You can see the nervousness in their eyes and body language. They just need to be told that they can do this. Start slow and run smart. They need what I once needed: that little boost of encouragement to take a deep breath, take courage, and start.

Years later and many marathons completed, I still find myself in need of that tiny nudge. I need the gentle touch on my shoulder that lets me know I don't have to face my fears alone. I need that soft whisper in my ear reassuring me that I can do anything I set my mind to. I need that text message that opens up the possibilities and encourages me to dream of something bigger than I would on my own. I need people in my life who believe in me when I start doubting myself.

As I look at the people I choose to keep close, I notice characteristics that are common between all of them. They have fiery passion for life. They are brave. They anticipate and welcome challenges. They are strong, so strong that they are able to lift up others around them while carrying their own burdens. They know who they are and what they want in life. They inspire me to be my best self.

Friends. It's a one-syllable word that encompasses a flood of emotions and brings to mind countless faces. While I toe the starting line all by myself and my finish time is all mine, I know that in my heart I am carrying bits and pieces of people with me every step of every race. I carry the knowledge that success or failure is immaterial in comparison to the love I receive from them. I know they will be supportive and proud of me for my effort, not my results. I know that our relationships are so deep and wide that if I fail, they will be there to soften the blow. And when I reach success, they will celebrate with me and brainstorm new ways to be better.

We are who we surround ourselves with. The voices of the friends we choose become the voices we hear in our heads when we struggle. I look at my friends and feel immense gratitude for who they are and the role they play in my life. And then I look in the mirror. Am I a good friend? Do I inspire my friends to be their best selves? Do I take the time to give a hug when they experience failure? Do I dare to share big dreams with them? Am I liberal with my compliments and stingy with my criticism? Is my voice in their heads one that will make them stand a little taller?

Family. It's a three-syllable word, and exponentially more important than friends. I look at my four beautiful, smart, and kind little people. Knowing that I am that voice in their heads is a heavy mantle I wear as their mother. But, it also is empowering to know that I can help shape the way my children view life.

Olivia, my only daughter and second child, is an avid swimmer. She has loved swimming since she could toddle and is in the water all day when we go to the beach or lake. The look of happiness on her face as she plays is priceless. As soon as she was able to be in a class setting and take direction from an instructor, I put her in swim lessons year-round. She progressed through the skill levels quickly and she eventually was invited to join swim team prep as a result of her dedication and practice. In swim team prep, she has to swim nonstop for an hour, utilizing different strokes. She is refining her technique and gaining fitness through hard work.

I picked Liv up from swim one evening and she seemed tired and distraught. When I asked how practice went, she said it was getting hard. It was still fun and she loves swimming, she told me, but it was getting more difficult. Recalling familiar feelings from marathon training, I could relate.

There a fine balance in healthy hobbies between work and play. Running is enjoyable, but at mile 23, it is hard. I want to be done. However, I also knew the sense of self-satisfaction that would eventually come to her if she persisted when it got hard. My job as a mother isn't to protect my children from challenges in life, it is to prepare them. I want Liv to have grit so when she meets an obstacle, she won't view quitting as an option.

This was much bigger than swim. This was a character-defining moment that would parlay into other areas of her life. It was time to talk. I wanted to look into her big sparkly blue eyes when I spoke. My personality isn't soft and cuddly. I am blunt and direct. I utilize compassion and empathy, but my children know when I am passionate about a topic. I pulled my car over and I asked Liv if she intended to quit everything in life when it got hard. She had wanted to make the swim team for years and had worked so hard to get into swim team prep. She was on the cusp of realizing a dream and goal she had set for herself years prior. I studied her face, watching her reaction to see how best to communicate and how far to push the conversation.

I pulled the mirror down from the sun visor and told her to look at her reflection. Did she see the face of a quitter? Or did she see the face of someone who was going to work hard and get stronger? Did she want to keep improving until she could make the swim team or did she intend to quit every sport when it required hard work? I told her that this conversation was much larger than running and swimming. It was a lesson in life. Life is going to be hard. There are going to be times when we really want to quit. Sometimes that's the best thing for us, and sometimes it's not. I didn't care if she quit swimming, I just didn't want her to become a quitter in life. I was willing to accept many reasons for quitting swim, but because it was "hard" was not on the list of reasonable excuses. When life is hard, we have to look at ourselves in the mirror and ask if we're going to work harder or quit.

I scooted over to where she could see my face in the reflection alongside of hers. Her big blue eyes were fixed on my green eyes. I was in her personal space and that made her smile with wonder. We stared at each other for a minute as the words sunk in. I pointed at my face and told her that the lady in the mirror chose not to quit when life got hard. I told her that when I am running I get tired. I hurt. I want to stop. It isn't easy for me either. I also told her that I finish what I start and that I am not afraid of hard work. Hard work gives me grit and the confidence to know that I can do whatever I set my mind on. Then, I pointed at her face in the mirror and asked her what that lady was going to do.

We sat in the car, cheek to cheek, staring at the mirror as a long silence hung in the air. Her light blue eyes, framed with their long black eyelashes, stared back at me. I looked at her face and saw a sprinkling of freckles on her round cheekbones. I looked at that little girl and knew that if she learned how to work hard, especially when life got hard, she had so much potential. She is amazing. I knew that her personality would allow her to do anything she wanted, but she needed to know that or her talents would go unfulfilled. Just between her sweet little round cheeks I saw the corner of her lips start to turn upward. Her blue eyes started dancing to the music of her giggle.

Turns out Olivia isn't a quitter either. Liv is going to keep swimming. When she gets tired, she will have to ask herself if she is a quitter or a finisher. When life gets hard for her, she will hear my voice in her head telling her that she can do it. She might remember staring in the mirror cheek to cheek as we both decided what kind of women we were going to be. When she is faced with a challenge, I wanted her to know that I believe in her. I will be that small voice in her head assuring her that quitting just because something is hard is not in her DNA.

Friends. Family. The voices in your head. They inspire us to be stronger than we think we can be. They plant the seeds of dreams that bloom and flourish into goals. They give us the tiniest of nudges that can help us get back on course, that correct our steering and point us toward the right path. When the world is quiet and my soul is at peace, I think about the text message from my friend. I think about the advice I received from a loved one. And then I take those thoughts on a run, my way of providing soil and sunshine for those seeds of dreams to start putting roots down and grow.

KINDNESS

"When we seek to discover the best in others, we
somehow bring out the best in ourselves."

—*William Arthur Ward*

With three little kids in tow, I headed into the grocery
store for some basic necessities. I had a small window for a
quick trip between the big kids' nap and the baby's nap and
feeding. Just milk, yogurt, fruit, and a little bread, enough
to survive until the weekend when I could do my usual
thorough shopping trip without the kids.

Parenting three small children, as anyone who's done it
knows, was physically and emotionally exhausting. House
chores and my job were also heavy demands on my energy.
I tried to make our free time as fun as possible, spending it
out of the house together on things we enjoyed rather than
errands. That day, though, a grocery trip was essential.

The kids were all so small, it was easiest to put them inside the shopping cart instead of letting them wander around touching everything on the shelves. With them sitting in close proximity, there was a fair amount of elbowing, pushing, and bugging one another. With a five-year-old, a two-and-a-half-year-old, and a newborn in a car seat carrier my cart was full of kids before I even started adding food. I was worn out and in a hurry to get everyone home, short on room in my shopping cart and patience in my heart.

At our local store the bakery will give kids a cookie to eat while parents shop. I try to finish my shopping by the time the kids have nibbled them down. Carefully placing the milk jugs on the bottom of the cart, the fruit and bread where it was least likely to get squished, and all the rest of the groceries on top of my kids' legs, I swiftly shopped as my children happily ate their snacks. We reached the checkout just as they were finishing their cookies and becoming restless. As they began to aggravate each other, I began to lose my patience with them. They wanted out of the shopping cart, but having children wander around the store would surely exhaust the remaining patience I did have. I, too, was ready to get home.

The checkout line seemed to take forever, at least long enough for my kids to start poking, squirming, and complaining about being underneath groceries and confined so close to one another. I was frustrated with the unbearably slow line and anxious to finish our outing and get back into an environment where the kids could play and make noise without the judgment, stares, and comments of others. Life at the time was stressful with three small children, a demanding job I worked from home, and a husband who was absent due to work and school. I don't recall exactly why I felt exhausted and worn out that particular day, but it was a hard season and I recall the feeling of desperation vividly.

My patience had whittled away by the time the clerk was bagging my groceries. I was getting short with my children and my frustrations were rising. Dinner time was drawing near and the kids were both tired and hungry. I knew nothing could possibly get better until they were fed and could start winding down for the evening. However, I also knew things would probably just get worse based on how the day had been trending. With rambunctious kids and short patience, misery was my date for the rest of the evening. That was, until an act of kindness saved me.

From behind me, I heard a middle-aged gentleman call out my name. It was Mr. Walker. Short in stature, with peppered black and white hair, glasses, and a small belly hanging over his jeans, he had a welcoming and warm personality. Mr. Walker went to church with us and although we didn't associate closely, we were friendly acquaintances. He politely asked how I was doing, although I'm sure he could guess just by looking at me that I was more than a little stressed out. He spoke with my children and entertained them while the clerk continued ringing up the groceries.

A grandpa now, he knew how to relate to me and my children. He was kind, caring, and compassionate, with six kids of his own. He teased, played, and tickled the kids, instantly lightening their moods. Mr. Walker had already purchased his groceries and we both stood at the checkout line long after I had been cashed out, chatting while the clerk continued to ring up other customers. I was enjoying the adult conversation and the temporary distraction. As we turned to exit the grocery store, Mr. Walker asked which one of my kids wanted to ride on his shoulders. He swooped up my happy daughter and walked me to my car.

I was so grateful for the small bit of time he took out of his day to be kind to me. A smile, a caring word, and a friendly face buoyed my spirits. In the parking lot, I put the baby and his car seat into the car and buckled up my other kids. In the meantime, unbeknownst to me Mr. Walker had loaded my groceries. I could feel tears welling up in my eyes, knowing what a lifesaver he had been. I had entered the grocery store stressed and overwhelmed from a long day, but I left feeling happy and light. As Mr. Walker turned to leave, I expressed my gratitude and told him to tell Mrs. Walker hello for me. A smile crept onto his face as he admitted that he didn't really want to go home quite yet. I asked Mr. Walker why, curious about this comment from such a happy man—Mrs. Walker was as sweet and kind as he was.

Mrs. Walker might be a little upset that he had missed his youngest daughter's parent-teacher conference at the high school, he explained. A slow realization came over me. Mr. Walker had missed his daughter's conference because of the time he spent extending kindness to me and my children. Noticing my face as I mentally put the puzzle pieces together, he put his arm around my shoulder. He looked me in the eye as he slowly spoke to my heart. I cannot recall his specific words, but his message was this: "You needed my time more than my wife and daughter. They are fine and I could tell that my time spent helping you would be meaningful to you."

It's now more than six years later, and I still see Mr. Walker around our small community, driving down the street or walking with his wife. We occasionally pass each other in the halls at church. He gives me that same sweet smile and a soft hello each time. And every time, I find that I have tears in my eyes. When he lightened my burden in the grocery store many years ago, he permanently changed the way I view acts of kindness. Instead of waiting for grand moments, I now feel inspired to perform smaller acts of kindness when the need is just as great. Sometimes, the smaller the act, the bigger the impact. Sometimes it's as simple as being perceptive to the needs of others and willing to help.

Maturity has taught me that extending kindness to others is easy and the opportunities are abundant. When I get to see the smile on someone's face and the gratitude in her eyes, there's a warm feeling in my own heart as I realize that I have made a positive difference in another person's life. When a friend tells me about a bad race or is stressed or nervous before one begins, I can respond warmly with a hug and words of encouragement that have helped me in the past. Helping someone often takes very little effort from me, but may permanently impact another.

Not long ago I met a nervous new runner at a marathon starting line. From her jittery, nervous behavior, it was obvious she was a first timer. The first marathon is special. It sets the tone for future races and expectations, and will be tied to many memories. You never forget your first. Like first loves, first babies, first homes, and first cars, first marathons are no different. Every detail is relished. I could see the self-doubt in this woman's eyes as she looked around, and I saw myself in her, without the years of experience. I wanted to say so many things to her, but mostly I wanted to hug her and tell her to stop worrying. She would finish. I knew she would because I could see that the self-doubt was mixed with determination.

I walked up and said hello, trying to calm her nerves, offering a distraction at the very least. Mr. Walker had been a distraction for me, and a perfect one at that! I told her I knew she could do it. We talked about rookie mistakes like going out too fast or under- or over-hydrating. We made sure her shoes were double-knotted and her race bib was fastened. Just then, she realized her timing chip wasn't attached to her shoe.

She went into panic mode. She didn't remember seeing one in her race bag, or in her hotel room. She frantically looked for her cell phone to call her family to locate it for her. This was her first marathon, and without her chip there would be no record of her officially finishing the race.

Then it dawned on me. I grabbed her arm and asked if she had taken the chip off her race bib the night before. She looked at me, puzzled. I realized she didn't know that her timing strip was attached to the back of her race bib. I unfastened her bib, flipped it over, and there it was, still attached. I ripped off the timing strip, knelt down, and attached it to her shoe. I could feel her relax.

It wasn't much effort on my part. I didn't go much out of my way. However, as one experienced runner, I saw a need in another. And just like Mr. Walker—an experienced parent who saw another parent in need—all it took was a little bit of time and kind words. Had I not helped her, she would have run the race. She would even have received her time since the timing strip was attached to her bib—but she would have worried about it the whole way. Had Mr. Walker not stopped to visit with me, I too would have survived and life would have gone on. And yet Mr. Walker completely changed my mental state that day, and I've never forgotten it. Though I never saw her again, I think I may have done the same for that nervous new runner.

Extending kindness to others has been surprisingly easy. Showing kindness to myself has been much more difficult. When I have a bad race, I often get angry at myself, wondering what I could have done to have a better result. When I make a simple mistake, I have a tendency to mull it over in my head repeatedly. The words I let my head convey to my heart are not always positive and encouraging. When my body doesn't want to do what my mind wants it to, I get frustrated, full of doubt and uncertain of my abilities. But then, I have to remind myself that I wouldn't speak to a friend the same way I am speaking to myself. I deserve my own kindness. I deserve my own forgiveness. I deserve an occasional pass to fail. I had denied myself kindness that day in the grocery store, making a stressful shopping trip even more stressful. Looking back, I was doing the best I could. And, it was pretty darn good. Instead of praising myself for all I accomplished, I criticized myself for my perceived shortcomings. And, now that my kids are older, I doubt anyone in the store even cared if my children were a little cranky. They were, after all, small children nearing dinnertime and bed time.

Yes, sometimes I raise my voice at my kids. Sometimes I lose my temper. I forget obligations. I get too busy to return phone calls. I forget special events. I could be a better person. But instead of making a list of all the ways I fail to measure up to my own expectations, I am trying to focus on what I do well. My kids know that I love them. They are clean and fed. They are well-adjusted. I do remember friends' birthdays and try to make them feel special. I file my tax return on time. I am a charitable person. I certainly have failures, but I also have successes. I am trying to choose to forgive myself for my shortcomings, even as I resolve to try harder and do better next time. I have plenty of room for growth, but we all deserve a little kindness, and I want to keep looking for ways to show it—to others and to myself.

DETAILS

*"If you desire to make a difference in the world, you
must be different from the world."*

—*Elaine S. Dalton*

I am a nerd, a numbers girl, a Type A, OCD, and slightly
neurotic person. I would have to be to engage in this type
of goal, right? It's true, and I won't even bother denying it.
Since I am approaching middle age, I have started embrac-
ing who I am and not apologizing anymore. Instead, I find
myself gravitating toward others like myself. These are my
people, my tribe. I get inspired by them and am motivated
to be better by watching them work to achieve their goals.

When I hear of people's extraordinary accomplish-
ments, I am immediately hooked by the grand scale of what
they've done. I love learning about individuals who think up
extreme physical challenges, like swimming from Florida to

Cuba, or doing the Ironman distance repeatedly, or participating in long-distance road bike races. Numerous stories
have been written about people who run coast to coast or
along the western shoreline. These people let their imagina-
tions run freely as they decided how to challenge the human body's limits. Their creativity and sense of adventure
intrigue me. While I am amazed at their goals, I also have a
craving for the details: How did they do it? James Lawrence,
known as the Iron Cowboy, is someone I have looked up
to. A father of five, he did a full Ironman distance in all 50
states, over 50 consecutive days. I'm fascinated and inspired
by his ability to dream big and execute his goals while balancing those against the demands of day-to-day life.

I long to ask questions. How long did it take to plan?
To train and prepare? How much did it cost? Was your
family supportive? What went on behind the scenes that
assisted your training? What advice would you give someone trying for a similar goal? I want them to indulge me
with every morsel of detail so my mind can wrap itself
around the whole experience.

Running a marathon in every state has required a lot
of planning and training. I imagine that some people look
at this goal with the same amazement I've felt looking at
others' achievements. Because of this, I wanted to share
the details of this experience to show the time, effort, and
dedication that have gone into my adventure. While there
have been variations and adjustments along the way, I am
a creature of habit and my methods have now been finely
honed. These are MY details.

TRAINING

"Always bear in mind that your own resolution to succeed is more important than any one thing."

—*Abraham Lincoln*

When I first started running, I ran no more than 40 miles per week. Over the last decade, I have inched my way up to closer to 85 miles per week. However, I increased my miles slowly and gave my body time to adapt to the new demands. My weekly mileage has increased because the number of marathons I run per year has increased. In my earlier marathon days, I only ran two or three annually. Now I run between seven and 10 marathons per year, meaning I run more longer runs. Over the course of training to run a marathon in each state, I estimate I will have run more than 52,000 miles.

The circumference of the earth is 24,900 miles, meaning that in my training I will have run far enough to circle the earth twice, with enough miles left after that to run back and forth between the west and east coasts of the U.S. Surely, only an insane person would have run that much! Of course, my weekly mileage fluctuates. As I've gotten older, I have added weight lifting and yoga to my schedule, which cuts into my running time. I also have to modify based on family demands. With four busy kids and a husband who regularly travels for work, I often have to push and shove miles around in my week. I try to be consistent while leaving room for flexibility.

Aside from the nine or 10 hours I spend running each week, I also spend approximately five hours a week doing research for my races. Assuming a total of 15 running-related hours each week, that means I spend about 780 hours each year planning and running marathons. I run every day of the year including holidays, weekends, and vacations (which are my favorite times to run). Extrapolating from the first marathon I ran in September of 2003 through the final marathon I have scheduled for October 2017, my running and marathon-related time investment will total nearly 13,000 hours, considering running, researching, planning and traveling to the marathons. It's important to note that this is my hobby; it isn't "work" for me. I love it and can't wait to research my next adventure. I find time when the kids are playing in the bathtub, while I wait in the line at carpool pick-up, while the kids are at swimming lessons, and often while I am in the airport traveling home from a race. Part of the excitement I feel for each marathon comes from doing the research and thinking about the possibilities.

GEAR

The experts say that shoes are good for roughly 500 miles and that running on old shoes will lead to injuries. Running on the wrong type of shoe will also cause injury. I'm lucky that my feet are average and my body is low maintenance. New Balance is the brand that keeps my feet happy. Thanks to the internet, I can buy shoes through discount wholesalers on year-end closeouts, using great sale prices and free shipping to purchase shoes in bulk. In my closet at home there are usually four to six pairs of running shoes in rotation. My upper shelf is filled with shoeboxes waiting on deck. My closet space is reserved for my regular clothes, but my dresser drawers are carefully organized to fit my running clothes. I have two drawers for tops: short sleeves and tank tops for summer running and long-sleeved shirts for winter running. I have a drawer for running socks, another drawer for sports bras, and two drawers for bottoms: skirts and shorts in one drawer and capris and pants in another. Everything is carefully organized so I can easily see what I have and grab it quickly in the morning when I am rushing out the door (or, when I'm feeling prepared, laying things out the night before a run). My shoes are the easiest part of my wardrobe because they are consistently the same model. I have invested roughly $4,000 in shoes and clothing for this project.

EXPENSES

Each race totals between $500-750 for the airfare, hotel costs, race fees, and minor miscellaneous expenses. Over the course of the entire project my race expenses will total nearly $32,000. I usually use reward points to mitigate the cost of airfare and hotel charges. When I total everything—travel, gear, etc., I have easily invested $40,000. Because I am not an elite athlete with sponsorships, the expense comes out of our family budget. Fortunately, my husband and I are both CPAs and we budget well. I know that I will spend about $5,000 per year on race-related expenses and my husband is wise enough to know that $5,000 annually is a bargain for a happy and sane wife. With dual incomes for the majority of this adventure, it was fairly easy to carve out a piece of our income for my hobby. As I transitioned into being home full time, I negotiated with my husband for my annual race expenses to stay in the budget. Everyone needs a release. Some people golf, drink, gamble, shop, dine out, or vacation. I race. Compared to other forms of entertainment, running is a relatively cheap and healthy alternative. Luckily, my husband has always been supportive and understanding.

NUTRITION

Calories burned are based on body weight and how efficient the body has become at any given activity. A woman of my size will burn roughly 90-100 calories per mile. My total of 52,000 miles equates to a lot of Peanut M&M's and no-bake and pumpkin cookies. I suffer from the "garbage disposal" effect after a long run or marathon, eating everything in sight. I don't diet, which I've written about separately, and until recently I have not used supplements or oils. Aside from my sweet tooth and my Diet Coke addiction, I identify mostly with the idea of eating clean and unprocessed foods, believing that everything our bodies need can be found easily in unprocessed foods, most of them accessible in the average grocery store. I try to eat healthy most of the time, but I gravitate toward food based on how it makes me feel. If I feel like eating a bagel, I know my body needs carbs for energy. If my stomach is bloated, I like to eat more fiber through fruits and veggies. Protein is always necessary, so I try to eat some good sources of that every day, like a salmon steak or a chicken breast. And because life is meant to be enjoyed, I will indulge in a cookie, spoonful of ice cream, or other sugary treat occasionally.

Deserving a paragraph of its own is my Diet Coke consumption. Diet Coke is the true hero of this adventure. Without it, this would not be possible. After each run, I hydrate immediately with a 52-ounce Diet Coke. While experts recommend various rehydration drinks such as chocolate milk, water, or electrolyte beverages, I prefer the carbonated and caffeine-heavy ice-cold cola. This is mostly because of my addiction to caffeine, adoration of the taste, and extreme thirst. My stomach doesn't handle digestion well before or during a race, so I am parched when I finish a long run or marathon. Diet Coke always hits the spot. Often, my stomach will remain sensitive long after my run is finished, so I will continue to drink soda for hours. The carbonation fills my stomach and the caffeine gives me a jolt of energy. I conservatively estimate that I have consumed over 850,000 ounces of Diet Coke as hydration over the 14 years from this project's beginning to end. I used to drink Diet Coke in cans and plastic bottles until I convinced my husband to purchase a soda fountain dispenser for the garage. It is perfectly chilled and always ready for consumption.

SCHEDULE

I get up between 4:30 and 5:00. I am the kind of runner who can roll out of bed, throw my hair in a twisty, and be out the door within five minutes. Often, I am meeting a group of girls at the bottom of the hill I live on, and I value punctuality. We usually start running at 5:00. I run until 6:30, knowing as soon as I blast through the door back at home, it's time to hang up my running shoes and be mom. During the school year, I am on a very tight schedule. After finishing the run at 6:30, I give myself 15 minutes to say goodbye to the girls, drive up the hill, and get in the shower. I pass my husband putting on his shoes before heading into work as I am quickly sliding my running shoes off. Experience has taught me that I need to be out of the shower at 7:00 in order to start waking the kids up for school. They slowly get out of bed, get dressed, brush their hair and teeth, make their beds, and prepare for school until 7:20. By then, I have myself dressed, makeup on, and bed made. The kids eat breakfast from 7:20 until 7:40. While they eat, I dry and style my hair. Since I put my kids in various schools around the valley where we live, I have to pack their lunches and drive them to school every day. Having four kids out the door with packed lunches in hand by 8:00 is my post-workout speedwork.

The morning routine does vary at times. It used to be that a business trip for my husband meant I got to run the half-mile loop by my house so I could always be close to home, or I would run on my treadmill. As my children have gotten older and more independent, I have slowly eased into leaving them home alone in the mornings when my husband can't be there. This little bit of freedom, the ability to have my morning time to myself, has grounded me as life has become hectic.

I've adapted my schedule as my kids have gotten older. I'm very routine driven and my kids are clear about my expectations. Luckily, we have found a groove that works for everyone. During the summer months, I have a little more flexibility, but I usually stick to my early mornings. I like waking up before the world does. I enjoy welcoming the sun over the mountaintops, watching the dark sky turn to dawn and eventually full sunshine. The weekends might seem more forgiving, but that is when I do my long runs. My long runs are usually between 16-22 miles and take two and a half to three hours to complete. With four children and extracurricular activities, we are often darting out the house even on weekends at 8:30 for soccer games or weekend skiing. For me, early works best.

FLEXIBILITY

My running has been an evolution. It has been the ultimate experiment of trial and error. I know I can't eat before a run or during a run because I have in the past and it makes me sick. I know how much rest I need before a race and what my body needs for recovery. Over the years, I've tweaked every aspect of my training, nutrition, racing, and recovery until I know exactly what my body needs. For the first 38 marathons I didn't use a training schedule, consult a coach, or do speedwork as part of my training. I have incorporated those changes recently because my goals have shifted. I have gotten older and my body is different than it was 14 years ago. It's the same with nutrition. As a younger runner I was able to be more flexible with my diet and my body would recover well. As I have aged, my needs have changed. My mileage increased and as a result the nutrients I need have shifted.

Life is a constant juggling act. Knowing that the balance is shifting as I age, adjust my goals, and change as a runner, I realize the importance of monitoring the physical needs of my body. I've learned to listen to the signs it gives me. I know that if I ignore them, my body will scream louder until I do. When my knees start to ache after a normal run I know that I need to replace my shoes. If my muscles are not recovering well, I add in some cross-training like yoga, spin class, or hiking. And sometimes, I reduce mileage if that is what my body needs. After tough workouts and races, I will schedule a deep tissue massage to push the toxins out of my muscles. The body, if listened to, will tell you what it needs. Running is my release and I try not to make it complicated. Aside from my music, I run free of burdens and distractions.

Sacrificing time, money, energy, and sleep is a small price to pay for the benefits offered from running. It's a beautiful and wild life. I wouldn't change a thing! What I have gained has been so valuable. Each morning, I find myself slipping out of my bed at that early, dark hour, lacing up my shoes, and hitting the pavement. I don't feel guilt for the time away or the money spent chasing my dreams and indulging in my hobbies. Experiences shape who we are, not the money we save or the time we waste. Running is my calm in this crazy world, and that is priceless.

FRIENDSHIPS

"Don't walk behind me; I may not lead
Don't walk in front of me; I may not follow
Just walk beside me and be my friend."

—*Albert Camus*

Sometimes I hate her, but she is my best friend. She knows me better than anyone. I confide to her all my deepest thoughts and feelings. She knows what the pause in my response and the scrunch in my brow mean, and often gives me the words that seem stuck in my throat. She knows my strengths and my weaknesses, ambitions, and insecurities. She knows what to say when I doubt myself. When I need to be inspired, she is always there.

There are a lot of reasons to love her. She is amazing—loyal, funny, smart, understanding, reliable. Anyone would be lucky to have her as a friend. Yes, sometimes I hate her. But the reason I hate her is because she seems to know me better than I know myself. She is unwilling to let me take the easy road. She is honest with me. Brutally honest, sometimes. I tell her I am not good enough. I express doubt. She won't listen to any of it. I find it so frustrating when she dismisses my hesitations. For all of that, I get angry. But, then again, that is also why I love her so much.

We have run together nearly every day for the last seven years. When I moved into her neighborhood, she was one of the first people to welcome me. She spotted me outside sweeping my driveway and came over to introduce herself. We began running together shortly after. The days turned to weeks, months, and eventually years. We became so connected to each other's lives, it seemed as if we had been friends forever. We leaned on each other through tough times and we celebrated successes. The friendship born in running permeated the rest of our lives.

Her name is Vicki. I love that she is the most dedicated, hard-core competitive person I have ever met. One morning on a run about two years ago she asked me where my running was going. I wasn't sure what she meant by that; I always had a marathon to look forward to and was in the middle of working toward my goal of running a marathon in each state. But she didn't want to know what marathon I was doing next. She wanted to know to what level I would take my running.

I had already qualified for the Boston Marathon, the world's most prestigious race. In 2008 I won the Spokane Marathon's women's division. I had won a couple of half marathons and qualified to run as an elite runner in nearly

every race I entered. I didn't have many specific goals beyond finishing strong. Even so I generally placed among
the top three females when I raced, and I almost always
finished in the top three in my age group. As long as I felt
good about my effort, I was content.

Vicki wasn't content. "You have so much more potential than you know," she said that morning. "I want to lay
a new goal upon you." She told me that she didn't want me
to respond, just to think about what she was going to tell
me. She said that she believed I was good enough to qualify for the Olympic Trials. My dedication, endurance, and
natural ability had already pushed me to results I'd never
expected, she said, and I still had room for improvement.
She knew I could do this.

I nearly choked on my laughter! I was a self-taught runner. At the time, I had never used a formal training plan,
rarely did any speedwork, and, only occasionally ran hills
depending on my mood. I had always felt like an imposter
in running and marathoning. I didn't really know what I
was doing beyond the tips I'd found in books and magazines and on the internet.

But Vicki wasn't joking. She probed me about my long-
term running goals, and then she did what I hate most. She
kept asking questions, even after I told her I was not willing to dedicate the time or energy required for Olympic-
level fitness. She asked why I wasn't taking my running to
the next level. For her it was clear: since I'd already qualified for Boston years before, the next level would be trying
to qualify for the Olympic Trials. But that was too far out
of my comfort zone, and something I didn't think I was

capable of. I told her that I was being realistic, that I was content with my goals.

But over the following years, I did become more serious about my running. Wanting to get faster, I increased my speedwork, tightened my nutrition, and started thinking about properly preparing my whole body for hard racing. And like a perfect drip system, Vicki would randomly and consistently remind me that she thought I could run fast enough to qualify. As my personal record for the marathon dropped, she never failed to remind me of my potential.

And now I find myself hiring a coach to train me for the Olympic Trials. This is why sometimes I just hate her. Vicki pushes me out of my comfort zone. I factor in my own perceived limitations. I give myself excuses to pull back. I am scared of the mountain in front of me. But she doesn't feel those emotions. She sees my capability and knows my dedication and work ethic. Where I see my limitations, she sees my potential.

Vicki is just one of the amazing running friends in my life. Running friends are different than casual friends. Casual friends might see each other in the grocery store or at a soccer game and catch up for a few minutes in passing. Perhaps closer friends might spend an evening out together every couple of weeks. A running friend, by contrast, gets an hour every day and more on the weekends. The depth of the friendship can be heard in the endless hours of talking and felt in the comfortable silence.

My running friends and I know the intimate details of each other's lives. We've spent so many hours together that when we ask a question, we hear the unspoken words hidden in the silent pause and the self doubt that fills the hesitations. Our friendships take on exceptional depth and meaning for two reasons. First, we have time to share the boring details that don't ordinarily come up with other friends. I tell my girls how I am cleaning out closets today or that I have a dentist appointment. They know what happened yesterday, what is happening today, and what will happen tomorrow. And because they are so close to the details of my life, they are often the first responders when a time of need arises, big or small. They offer to help because they know I need it. Many times I have been in a pinch with shuffling kids and one of them will help me with carpooling, or offer to run an errand on my behalf. And I reciprocate. We are able to do this because we are intimately connected. Second, I find that not only do I share the boring daily details of my life, but I also share the deepest secrets of my heart.

With a solid friendship foundation, I can share my past, my current struggles, and my future worries without fear of judgment. I can seek their advice, knowing that they understand the frame of mind I come from and what I intend for an outcome. Countless times we have shared family struggles or personal dilemmas with one another, seeking a quorum of experts to brainstorm the best possible solution. These women have become my most trusted advisors.

Friendships born on the running trail are strong. They are deep. They are more meaningful than any other friendships I have made. Running edifies my physical body, but the friends I run with edify my mental, spiritual, and emotional self. They are priceless and irreplaceable. The friendships I have made through running remain strong even when we're no longer able to run together, like when someone moves to another town. The tie is so strong it can't be broken.

I am moving across the state soon. Vicki is moving to another state at the same time. While we will miss seeing each other every day, our friendship is now so deep it won't really change on many levels. She knows me. And I know her. We will still share our dreams and secrets with each other. When we no longer live in the same place we will travel to see each other. We'll exchange texts and emails and phone calls. Vicki is someone I will always have in my life. But I'll miss the intimacy that came from our daily runs. Best friends are not replaceable, but they are collectable. I know that there are other women out there who I will meet. They will inspire me in their own ways. And I know that I will fill a little hole in their hearts. We will find each other, just as soulmates always do.

THE FINISH LINE

*"What great thing would you attempt if you knew
you could not fail?"*

—*Robert H. Schuller*

Twenty-six point two miles is the official distance of the marathon. Ancient Greek history tells us that Pheidippides, born circa 530 B.C., was a courier who was sent to Sparta to warn of a battle at Marathon, Greece, where the Persians were invading. Pheidippides ran about 150 miles over two days. He rested and then ran a final 40 kilometers from Marathon to Athens to announce Greek victory in the Battle of Marathon. Immediately after relaying the message of a victorious battle, Pheidippides collapsed and died. That final 40K he ran has now become the marathon distance. The challenge is to finish better off than the original marathon runner.

When I ran my first marathon in the fall of 2003, I was convinced that Pheidippides and I would share the same fate, but I not only made it, but chose to race again and again. Over the miles I've learned so much more than how to run a marathon. As I think about the sweat, discouragement, failure, perseverance, determination, and successes, I am flooded with emotions. I feel excitement over the challenges I was able to gracefully face. I feel humbled by the lessons I had to learn the hard way. I feel inspired by those who helped me. I feel gratitude for my healthy body, my strong mind, and for my opportunities. I feel enriched by the experiences I have had, and recognize that they have created a depth in my being that I doubt would have developed otherwise.

Yes, I've had better luck than Pheidippides. My marathon experiences have not been the end of my story. The finish line of each has been more like the period at the end of a sentence. Each marathon represents a different chapter, capturing a piece of my life at a defined point in time. Each marathon finish brought me one step closer to the ultimate finish line of my goal to run a marathon in each of the 50 states.

I remember so vividly running the final stretch of my first marathon. The air was crisp on that fall morning. The sun was shining brightly and the air was still. I turned a corner and saw the banner that read FINISH LINE in big, bold letters. The finish line represented much more than accomplishing a physical feat. It represented the unknown, the unattainable, a possibility, and a dream. I knew that if

I could run a marathon, with enough knowledge, persistence, hard work, and determination, I could do anything I wanted to.

In every race, the last mile of the marathon triggers a split between my mind and my body. I'm filled with anticipation to see the finish line, to taste the victory, the reach the completion of a physically exhausting event. But, to get there, there's one more grueling, hard, long mile to run. Roughly 4,200 more steps on already exhausted legs. Every time, dread and excitement simultaneously fill my body. I turn to self-talk. I can't quit now; I've come way too far. I've worked too hard to give up when the end is in sight. Finding the physical and mental energy to continue is a fight.

And then, at last, there's the relief I feel when I cross the finish line, knowing that I was able to succeed once again. This is a feeling I now crave. The sweetness that comes with hard work and success is a taste my palate has grown accustomed to, and it has become a steady part of my diet.

But somewhere underneath this superficial feeling of satisfaction is another feeling brewing in my heart. Finding the proper adjectives and verbs to describe it is difficult because of the variety of emotions blending into one unsettling feeling. This feeling is familiar, one I've known outside of running as well. It's the sense of emptiness that starts to creep into my body as the end draws near. It's easier to stay motivated when there is still something to reach for, stretch for, attain. But when I finally get to the finish line, I momentarily feel content and then realize I've been chasing an illusion. The illusion that this time, I'll leave feeling complete and satisfied.

Will I ever be satisfied? Will I continue to chase a feeling that I will never be able to capture? Or is that the beauty of dreaming big, that nothing ever fills that space where curiosity and adventure reside? Is that the gene in my DNA that will keep pushing me to dream big and keep reaching beyond my perceived limits? I don't know what's coming in my racecourse of life. I don't know what hills I might face, however steep and long they might be. My speed may increase as I appreciate the ease of being well prepared, or perhaps I will slow to a walk when the course gets too challenging. Running marathons has taught me to keep moving forward, to press on to that finish line, whatever lies ahead.

I realize that I've only begun this journey of self-discovery. It wasn't the finish line that drew me to the marathon, after all. It was the miles along the way, in training and in racing, that were the most meaningful. With renewed confidence and perspective, I will now close this chapter of my life. I'll turn the paper to find a blank page. I will get to write new sentences with new periods, forming paragraphs that will accumulate to make another story in my book of life. And while I can't see the final finish line from where I stand now, I trust that I will keep learning and growing as I make my way there.

I crave the next adventure. The way won't be easy, but along the bumpy road, I know I will learn more about myself, and I will get stronger. And therein lies the beauty of this experience: here I stand on the top of a summit, and instead of feeling complete, I see another summit. It is higher and steeper—and I know that I will have an even better view once I get to the top. My hope is that from there I will see yet another mountain I want to climb.

SELF LOVE

Once when I was running,
from all that haunted me;
to the dark I was succumbing-
to what hurt unbearably.

Searching for the one thing,
that would set my sad soul free.

In time I stumbled upon it,
an inner calm and peace;
and now I am beginning,
to see and to believe,
in who I am becoming-
and all I've yet to be.

- Lang Leav

A LITTLE GLIMPSE

How do you juggle it all? This is the question I'm asked most often about running. As a busy mom of four kids, the logistics get complicated quickly. When you layer on a job at times, a traveling husband, and LIFE, making time for myself while taking care of my responsibilities is a feat in multitasking. I am an ordinary mom of four busy, involved, and growing kids. Just before a random Wednesday, I decided (literally the night before, so I could give a truly random sample of my schedule) that I would document my day to provide a glimpse of how I fit it all in. While my day is fairly ordinary (for those of us who call managing random and hectic family schedules ordinary), I hope it will inspire you to find time in your own life to pursue a passion.

A couple of caveats: First, this schedule has been tweaked and fine-tuned over the years. At this point, it's like a well-oiled machine. It works for me because I am organized, efficient, and a good multitasker. These are deep-rooted aspects of my Type A personality that have been honed over many years of parenthood as well as my professional experience managing people and projects. Second, today, happens to be a look at my life during a time when my husband is working in a different city. He will be notably absent from my day-to-day. As his job has gotten more demanding, his travel has increased as have his work hours. Because of the unpredictability that comes with his job, I don't depend on his help with my daily schedule. With that said, welcome to my random Wednesday.

4:30 – The buzz of my iPhone's alarm clock from beneath my pillow never fails to shock my nerves and jolt me out of bed. I know I have time to hit the snooze button at least once. I don't know why I don't just set my alarm for 15 minutes later and get up when it goes off. Trying to reason with my foggy brain at this hour is futile.

I typically set my clothes out on the bathroom counter the night before, which really helps. If I had to think about the temperature or picking out a top and bottom that don't look hideous together at this early hour, I would stand confused in my closet for a solid 30 minutes. I grab my clothes and slip them on while I finish waking up, struggling a bit to complete this challenging task. It's dark; no one will notice if my clothes are inside out or backward…I think?

I quickly brush my teeth, take a bathroom break, and head downstairs.

5:00 – I grab my supplements (a handful of multivitamins, fish oil, cranberry oil, iron, B-12, magnesium, fiber, calcium, and flax seed oil) and my pre-workout BCAA (branch chain amino acid) drink as I slip my shoes on. That is a fist full of chemicals, right!?! While I used to shy away from supplements, the nutritionist I have hired tells me that I need to replace vitamins my body is deficient in to remain healthy. I've consulted the family pharmaceutical rep, the family pharmacist, and the family doctor (and by family, I mean those family members I can squeeze for free advice). It all checks out and is supposed to keep this machine ticking…so I gulp them down! Strangely, just going down the stairs, I lost five minutes of my precious morning time. The clocks in my house are all slightly off, and instead of fixing them, I choose to remain completely surprised each morning when I make the realization that if I don't pick up my pace, I will be late! I jump in the car to meet this morning's running friends at our designated meeting spot.

5:15 – To be honest, as much as I value punctuality, I am always at least two minutes late. I don't mean to be, but I am. So, let's call this 5:17. I tie my shoes (reaching down toward my feet doubles as my pre-workout stretch). And we are off! Who I'm with, where we meet, and how far I go vary daily and adjustments are often made during the run itself. I have some friends who can only run early in the morning before work and others who want to stay in bed as long as possible. Accommodating all the friends along the way makes for an interesting route. Fortunately, I have run in Liberty Lake for over 10 years, and I know the route and distance between any two points like the back of my hand. Although math is my strength, calculating distance, pace, and duration in the early morning hours is challenging. One friend insists on a bathroom break at mile four, another refuses to get up before 6:00, and another needs to be home before 6:30. Since I love them all, I try to organize a route to include everyone, picking up and dropping off friends along the way.

I'm lucky and cursed. Lucky in that I can always find a friend to run with me. (I might need to adjust my distance or speed depending on the friend.) Cursed that since I run every day, I am the unofficial organizer. Most of my running friends check in with me to see what my plans are and who I am running with, and I include as many as possible. However, all of my friends know that I have a lot of random bits of info floating around in my head. I make mistakes and miss meeting places at times. But, forgiveness and unconditional love are two requirements for my friends. There are typically six of us who run together and have over the years. I used to run with a larger group, but the logistics got to be overwhelming. I like my friendships to be fewer and more intimate.

Tuesdays and Thursdays are speedwork days, but that doesn't work for everyone because certain girls don't like to run fast. On Fridays we run the hill and again, that doesn't work for everyone because not everyone likes to climb. Saturday is long run day, and most of us go different distances. It is often comical how much work goes into meshing all of our schedules, but that is what friends do, and so we make it work. On this particular morning, after

10 miles I am done catching up with my sweat sisters. It is time to head home and start the day with my kids.

6:45 – I have to be home no later than 6:45 or I will throw our whole day off. When my kids were smaller, my husband didn't travel as much and I could count on him being home in the mornings should anyone need parental help. As the kids got older and my husband started traveling more for work, I hired a neighbor girl to come sleep on the couch so I could run. Just this last year, I have felt comfortable enough leaving my kids home alone. We live in a safe neighborhood within a safe community. My kids have iPads and they know how to FaceTime or text me if they need anything.

So, back to my sweaty self, coming in from a run. I stink! And, my sweat is making me cold. I hate being cold so I jump in the shower, quickly yet thoroughly scrubbing the sweat off in 15 minutes. Picture not included due to graphic material! You're welcome.

7:00 – If I have only shaved one leg by this time, it doesn't matter, I must go! The other leg will get shaved tomorrow. I hustle out of the shower, clothe myself, and put on my makeup. This doesn't take more than 15 minutes. As I stuff myself into my clothes for the day (which I also set out the night before), I utilize my mother's way of waking up the kids: Yell at them. Repeatedly and loudly call their names until I get a response or hear their bodies moving around. It is completely annoying. It was when I was a kid, and it still is. However, it is effective and, more importantly, doesn't require me to do anything other than a little lung work.

The children know that they are responsible for some of their own personal care. They get dressed, make their beds, brush their teeth, fix their hair, and tidy up their rooms without my intervention. I do my daughter's hair, but she is responsible for brushing it and having her hair accessories ready. I give the boys a quick rundown of their chores to make sure they are ready to go. Most importantly, I give them the old "sniff test" to check their general cleanliness and to verify that they really brushed their teeth. Dog breath means a second brushing (or first depending on whose opinion you trust)! During this time, I often remind them to grab whatever they need for that day's extracurricular activities. They are responsible for their own piano books, soccer cleats, swimsuits, etc. In years past, I had to be responsible for gathering their things, or at least supervising to some extent. But, in efforts to raise responsible human beings, I let them be in charge of that now. Responsibility is a skill that we have to grow into, but I was finally able to put my helicopter parenting skills aside and let them learn life's lessons the hard way through choices and consequences. Sure, my kid has gone to soccer practice in snow boots. Once. A forgotten water bottle? No one died. Lost swim goggles? See if there is a pair the swim club will let you borrow. Through that they finally learn to think ahead for their own needs.

7:30 – Time for breakfast! (The kids eat breakfast together and we try to eat dinner as a family—husband included when he is home.) I don't accommodate individual meal requests. I decide what the kids will be getting, and they all get the same thing. They have 20 minutes to eat while I head upstairs to dry and style my hair.

7:50-8:00 – I am dressed, showered, and ready for the day as I head downstairs to clean up breakfast. If I have been efficient, I may have time to unload the dishwasher or toss some laundry in the wash. As the kids grab their lunchboxes, backpacks, and any additional things they need for school, I rinse their bowls and plates, put everything in the dishwasher, and wipe the counters. I haven't gotten breakfast but am usually not hungry yet. I don't like to eat in a hurry, so I typically wait until after dropping the kids off at school.

Having four kids, I am unable to carpool since I fill a car with just my own. I also drive all my kids because they go to choice schools that don't provide bus transportation. Luckily, they are all in the same general direction and the start times are staggered enough that I can drop off and pick up everyone on time. This I count as one of my biggest blessings.

Buckle up and time to blast off! My passenger seat is stuffed with bags, backpacks, snack bags, my purse, DVDs for the TV in the car, and any other miscellaneous articles needed for the day. I open a Diet Coke as I take my mental victory lap. Ahhhhh…. I feel like a champion EACH. AND. EVERY. MORNING. I get those kids deposited at school on time. Honestly, I feel like a freaking rock star.

8:45 – Drop off is complete and we're back home. It is not preschool day, so I have my little buddy, my four-year-old, with me for the day. I need to do some laundry, pack some lunches for tomorrow (some of my kids go to a school where hot lunch is not offered and another one of my kids is a picky eater and prefers a cold lunch), do some clutter control, and most importantly, walk around and make sure each and every toilet in the house is flushed. I tidy up the kids' rooms, pick up jammies that were thrown on the floor, and try to get ahead of household tasks. Evan plays underfoot, painting, doing Play Doh, doing puzzles, coloring, or doing worksheets. Today, we also make boats out of Legos for our Peanuts figurines to float on. Meanwhile, I make myself a meal based around a protein like egg whites.

10:30 – Yoga is on the schedule today. I do yoga twice a week, once on a weekday and once on the weekend. During the weekday session, my littlest attends the kids club at the gym. Running tightens my body, but yoga provides a deep stretch that I love, and it helps me connect mentally, spiritually, and physically with my body. I love yoga, the inversions, the peaceful environment.

12:00 – The afternoon is reserved for fun! I like getting outside and playing with my kids when they're not in school, going on walks with friends, or even running errands right before I start school pick-up. Lunch is often eaten on the go, even for me and the littlest.

2:15 – I am still in my yoga clothes and need to go home to change. The little man has been asking for a red shirt (he needs new jammies and summer shorts also) and I need some fruit and veggies from the grocery store. It is so much easier to run errands with just one kid, so I get ready quickly and take care of those needs with Evan before picking up the big kids.

4:15 – Time to pick up the three older monkeys from chess club. My kids are nerds, but they are adorable nerds and I love them!

4:30 – I've got one hour to get the kids home, started on their homework, and ready for soccer practice and swim team. Sometimes they are starving for an early dinner and other times they just want a snack. My littlest one has been begging to make pumpkin cookies all day long, so today we make those and have them for a snack before soccer and swim. I have a rare evening out planned with one of my running partners, so dinner prep today is avoided since the kids will eat at Subway. This time of the night is crazy, each kid working on several different chores before we load up and head out again! Every night of the week is like this, just filled with different activities. In my earlier years as a mom, we weren't this busy. As my kids have gotten older and more involved, this has changed. Part of it is having so many kids. The other part is that I would rather they fill their time being active, learning skills and with friends, than not.

5:30 – Liv is off to swim team and Austin is at soccer practice. The littler boys play at the park during soccer practice. Since I have plans with a friend, our part-time nanny meets me and takes over the evening duties from there. I have an awesome babysitter, and when we need her she picks up where I leave off. On this particular night, I leave her a list of tasks for each kid. She follows my schedule and steps into my shoes seamlessly. So, from here, I will show you what I am doing and what my kids are simultaneously doing. She will feed them dinner, follow up on piano practice and homework, and make sure they all shower/bathe before bedtime.

6:45 –Tonight the kids eat dinner at Subway. While I prefer a home-cooked meal, some days just require that I hit the Easy button!

7:30 – Rub-a-dub-dub, all stinky kids in a tub! While the two older kids shower in their own bathrooms, the littler boys enjoy a good soak in bubbles. They have an assortment of toys and will stay in the tub for an hour if I let them. I enjoy having them in the same place, enjoying one another. On typical evenings, I use this time to do laundry (it's by my master bath), set out my running clothes, set out my regular clothes, wash my face, brush my teeth, and on occasion lay on the bed and read a book while the little boys are in earshot the whole time.

7:00-9:00 – A girls' night out does the heart good! I can't believe I created something so beautiful. I am not right brained, so the fact that I was able to produce something resembling art is shocking to me. The CPA in my head high fives the Monet in my heart. #Rockstar

8:00 – As kids always seem to do, everyone gets hungry and thirsty as bedtime approaches. I don't tolerate the in/out of bed game, so the kids are offered milk and/or a snack at 8:00. I (or tonight, Angi the babysitter) catch up on dishes and miscellaneous household chores while they eat. If they finish before bedtime, we draw, do puzzles, play games, or just mill around the house relaxing and coasting into our evening.

8:45 – I've had a little baby for most of the last decade and usually lay with my youngest until they drift off to sleep. This process can take a little or a lot of time depending on the night. When I'm at home, it's my favorite time of the day. The little ones are so sweet and they whisper (often very moist whispers) their love for me. My youngest still likes me to lay down with him at night, scratch his back, and sometimes sing his favorite song. I love this time of the night. I am not anxious for this phase to pass.

9:15-9:30 – On occasion, like tonight after I get home, I enjoy an Epsom salt bath to help recover my sore muscles. Or, if I have lingering chores, I will finish them. My older children go to bed and read until I turn their lights out when I go to bed. It is the first time all day when my house is quiet. The silence is calming and soothing, even if it is only for a short 15 minutes.

9:30 – I collapse into bed, grateful for a day spent with family and friends, doing what I love. The days often feel long, but the weeks quickly pass. I go to bed exhausted, but I love this feeling of being in my cozy bed in my warm home with people I love….and I drift off to sleep.

FREQUENTLY ASKED QUESTIONS

Do you work?

Yes and no. I am a CPA with my master's degree in tax accounting. I worked in the professional world for 11 years before I transitioned to being home full time. During those 11 years, I had three children. My last child was born shortly after I stopped working outside the home. I feel like I have been exposed to every possible work/family life balance. I worked full time in the office before having kids. When I had one child, I continued to work in the office but worked slightly fewer hours. After I had a second child I shifted to working mostly from home, only going in to the office for critical times like month end and quarter end and for larger projects.

Do you run every day?

I can count on one hand how many times I have missed a day of running. I just love the way it makes me feel. Most people take rest days, but I take easy days where my miles are fewer and my pace is slower. I also believe that when I don't feel well, a good run in the fresh air is just what my body needs. The most difficult time to run is when I have to catch a 6:00 a.m. flight for a marathon weekend. It is most difficult to set my alarm for 3:00 a.m.

I prefer to run outside, which means I have invested in some really great clothing and gear to allow me to be in winter conditions without getting hurt or cold. I have a treadmill for those few days when outside running isn't going to happen.

Were you always a runner?

Nope! I was a dancer as a kid and a cheerleader in high school. I didn't start running until after I had graduated from college and started working as a professional. I sat at a desk in a cubicle all day long. It was dark when I went to work and often dark when I got home. I missed fresh air and natural lighting. I also didn't like all of the sitting. I was drawn to running because it satisfied my cravings for something different.

You seem to do so much! How do you manage it all?

This is the hardest question to answer. I have always had a busy schedule. Growing up on a farm, we learned to multitask and work hard. In college, I often took the maximum credits allowed and was able to finish my degree quickly. I worked full time as I was getting my master's and worked while I had children. I am a busy person who likes to be going.

With that said, I am a firm believer that we all make choices. I make sacrifices to enjoy running, but we all make sacrifices for the things that are important to us. It's my preferences are different. While I enjoy running, I find watching movies and playing electronic games, for instance, to be painfully difficult. I choose to run during my personal relaxation time, while others choose different pastimes.

When was your first marathon? Last?

My first marathon was Top of Utah in September of 2003. I was so nervous! I was terrified that I wouldn't be able to finish or that I would finish with an embarrassingly slow time. Having never participated in a running event or even a running group, I had no idea what to expect. I didn't sleep for days leading up to the race.

My last marathons will be Saturday/Sunday races in New Hampshire and Maine. These are small states and there aren't a lot of marathons offered in either of them. Plus, they are about as far away from the west coast as I can get, making travel difficult. I put them off until I couldn't anymore!

Best time in a marathon?

I have slowly chipped away at my best marathon time. My first marathon was 3:33:30, which was a Boston Marathon qualifying time. I've had a few races where I bonked. But, every year I seem to slowly whittle down my best time. My fastest race to date has been the Rock 'n' Roll Marathon in Washington, D.C. My grandmother had just passed away. Two months previously, my grandpa had passed away. I was extremely close to both of them. I always called my grandma from the airport to catch up (and get travel tips). When I got to the airport, I reached for my phone and realized that she wouldn't answer. I had an emotional breakdown. I suppose you could say that in the D.C. marathon, I ran my emotions out.

What do you eat during a marathon? Do you prefer certain types of foods?

I am a big believer in trial and error. Each of our bodies responds differently to different energy sources. I don't like the energy gels and energy drinks. I find that some of the chews are too large to comfortably chew and breathe. I like sports beans the best.

Before a race, I will eat a banana and a bagel, although I typically don't eat before a run. I know that during races I will push my body harder and farther and I need more fuel to finish strong. I try to stay well hydrated the day before and morning of a race. I prefer to eat as little as possible on the course, so the more I can eat before I start running, the longer I can go without worrying about refueling. Typically, I won't start drinking until mile 14 or eating until mile 18.

Must-have products?

Music! I need an assortment of good music. I like fast music for the first hour, slower music for the middle hour, and then faster music for the final hour. I have a playlist on hand, but I like an assortment of Pandora stations. Comfortable clothes that don't chafe (and Glide!) are a necessity. It is hard to run in pain. Good shoes are also important. I have come to appreciate compression socks.

Worst race conditions?
There are a few race conditions that I find difficult. I am not used to heat or humidity, so any race where those are a factor is hard. It is cooler and drier in the Northwest where I train, so my body doesn't acclimate easily. In the winter months when I am layering up at home to train in freezing temps, a hot and humid race in the Southern states will shock my system.

I also find altitude running difficult. When the air is thin my body gets dizzy from altitude sickness. Since it takes a few days for the body to adjust to altitude and I usually don't have that much time available in my travel schedule, I generally end up running these marathons feeling lightheaded. It is hard to focus and push your body when you don't feel normal.

How do you find the motivation?
I love pushing myself to see how well I can do. I love the feeling of accomplishment. Knowing my kids are watching me is my biggest motivating source. I try to be a good role model for them, not only in fitness, but in life. It is extremely important for them to see me set goals and work hard. I want to inspire them to keep bettering themselves

at every stage of life. I want them to find passions that make them happy. This love and drive motivates me to get out and run each day.

Do you ever not feel like running?

No. If I didn't want to, I wouldn't. To me, it is like sleeping and eating. My body needs it and craves it. Sometimes it craves more and sometimes it craves less, but it always needs sweat therapy.

How often do you buy new shoes?

The rule of thumb for running shoes is to have two pairs to rotate. The cushion in a shoe sole won't fully rejuvenate from day to day, so alternating with another pair is recommended. It is also recommended to retire a pair of shoes after 500 miles. I am sure all of this derives from many careful scientific studies. I prefer to just listen to my body. When my knees and hips start getting a little tender, I know it is time for new shoes.

I like to buy my shoes from discount shoe websites (when I find a model that works for me I'll buy eight pairs at once). I always have a stash of shoes in my closet that I can grab the morning I decide I need a new pair.

Who is your inspiration?

I get starstruck by elite runners like Shalane Flanagan, Kara Goucher, Grete Waitz, Deena Kastor, and others who are amazingly talented. I am in awe of their natural ability and discipline. It is fun to watch them compete and crush races. I love how social media has allowed us to see into professional runners' lives and get tips from them.

I am inspired even more by the everyday athlete. One man known as the Iron Cowboy, James Lawrence, has broken several world records and is always doing some insane physical feat. I identify more with the everyday guy who balances life and athletic goals because that is also my life.

I would be remiss not to mention a pioneer in women's athletics, Kathrine Switzer. It must have taken a lot of courage to run the Boston Marathon without identifying herself as female. She opened the door for people like me to be able to race. There were a lot of women like her that I am grateful for. I can now run the streets of my neighborhood without judgment or criticism because they pioneered the way for me and runners like me to engage in this sport.

Have you ever been injured?

Knock on wood, no, I haven't. My body gets sore and I will adjust physical activity based on my needs, but I have been incredibly lucky to avoid injury. After a marathon I will increase yoga to stretch my muscles. If I start to feel tight or sore, I will increase cross-training to strengthen my overall strength. I try to do a lot of preventative care to avoid injury, but mostly I am just lucky.

Have you run with each pregnancy?

Yes, I ran with each pregnancy up to the day I delivered my babies. I would run slower and fewer miles, but I needed to run for mental health. I had to be extra cautious not to trip and land on my stomach. I hydrated and listened to my body extra carefully during this time. Growing a healthy baby was my priority, but I felt like I could run and be pregnant simultaneously and safely.

I ran a marathon while pregnant with three of my kids. With two of the pregnancies, I was about 10 weeks along and didn't know I was pregnant yet. With my last baby, I was four and a half months along. Thankfully, all of my kids were born healthy and strong. While I was able to run and have healthy pregnancies, I would have stopped running if there was any issues with the development of my baby.

How many races do you do a year?

Running marathons is a hobby that I fit around the rest of my life. There have been periods when I am able to run a lot of marathons in a year (my max annual number is 10). There were other times when I didn't run a marathon for several years because I had a lot of really little babies and we moved three times in two years. Life happens!

As I have traveled to run marathons, a challenge has been to find good flights. The marathons in the South and Northeast are very difficult to get to and usually require an extra day because of the multiple legs, layovers, and losing time traveling east. I try to balance this with family life and my other obligations so I am not gone too much too often.

What training plan do you use?

When I first started running marathons, I wasn't sure what marathon training plan to use. I looked at several of them and noticed similar patterns. From that, I created my own. Oh, the ignorance and boldness! In a way, I am grateful I trusted myself from the beginning. That experience taught me to listen to my body and adjust based on how I feel. I like not being tied to a training plan.

Also, when I started running more marathons back-to-back, there simply weren't training plans to properly address my goals and schedule. I created my own and trusted myself, just like I had in the beginning. That skill I developed has served me well over the last 15 years because I have been able to run healthy without injury, and throughout all my pregnancies, while continually getting stronger and faster.

How much has this cost?

I haven't kept close track of the overall cost. I use frequent flier miles for cheap air travel and reward points for hotels whenever I can. I generally travel to races alone rather than with my entire family. With that said, I would guesstimate that travel expenses alone are $25,000. This expense has been incurred over 14 years, though.

This amount seems like a lot, but I haven't been to a primary care provider in over two decades. I don't have expenses related to poor health. (While I was employed outside the home, I didn't ever use a sick day.) Running is my hobby and my passion. Who can put a price tag on happiness?

Is your husband supportive? How do you get to leave so much?

This is easily one of the most frequent (and most annoying) questions I am asked. Call me a fully modern mom, but I don't view a weekend with dad as a treat or a huge baby-sitting favor. They are his children and he is their parent. While I try to make the weekends away easy by reducing the stress (frozen meals, babysitter to help out, arranging carpools with other parents, etc.), I also think it is good for him to regularly get a sample of what I do every day.

So, with that in mind, I will first ask what his work schedule is, then we will plan our family vacations. After work and family have been factored into the schedule, I will add in weekend races when it is most convenient. I am respectful of my family obligations and grateful for support, but I don't feel guilty for having personal time away.

Do your kids run?

Yes! My kids always want to join me in my runs. They will do the kids' races associated with marathons they are with me for. My older two kids joined track when it was offered at their schools. For now, since my children are so young, I mainly encourage them to have fun with exercise. My kids all play soccer and swim. I think it is important for them to enjoy exercising and to learn how to take care of their bodies.

Have you ever not finished a marathon?

Never. I am far too stubborn to quit. I would rather claw my way on my hands and knees across the finish line than not finish something I started.

Best race?

It is hard to pick a favorite; it's almost like picking a favorite child. I love them all for different reasons. They all teach me different lessons. With that said, I would say my most enjoyable experiences were Boston and NYC. Boston is a runner's marathon. It is magical and such an honor to be part of the most prestigious marathon in the world. I qualified on my first marathon, so I feel fortunate that I was able to race Boston early in my marathon running.

NYC was equally amazing. The racecourse, through the five boroughs, was really fun. I was there over Halloween weekend. We spent time in Central Park people watching, which is one of my favorite pastimes. New York is a fun city that is alive at all hours. The field of runners for the marathon is twice as big as Boston, and the logistics of the race was awe-inspiring. Of all the races I have done, New York and Boston are the two I most want to do again.

Worst race?

I experienced altitude sickness at the Steamboat Marathon in Colorado, making it very unenjoyable. I was so dizzy I felt like I had the flu the whole time. I remember laying down on a little grassy patch along the side of the road for 10-15 minutes around mile 18, wondering if I could go on. The only thought that kept coming to my mind was that if I didn't finish, I would have to come back and do it again. I wanted to go home so badly! Altitude sickness made me really sleepy, which added another level of difficulty.

The Hatfield McCoy Marathon in West Virginia is another of my least favorites. The race logistics made it very difficult. The start and finish of the race are in different locations, and there are so few lodging options that I had to stay about 20 minutes away from both the start and the finish. The course was very hilly and hot. The whole experience was much more stressful than fun.

How many miles per week do you run?
I started out with a goal to run five miles every day with the exception of my long runs (which would be varying lengths depending on my training cycle). At that point I averaged about 40-45 miles per week. I did this for a couple of years. As I started running more marathons in any given year (and my training cycles were shortened), I ran closer to 60-65 miles per week. Now, I average closer to 85 miles per week. I have seen my personal best marathon times decrease as my mileage has increased. There is a huge debate about running what are referred to as "junk miles," which some argue are not beneficial and can even be detrimental. On the other hand, some experts think that if you teach your legs to run when they are tired then they become stronger. All I know is my own results, and for me high mileage has been a good thing.

I think it is important to remember my running mantra: always listen to your body! If I feel rundown or tired I back off on mileage. I might also add in some cross-training when I feel fatigued. During the latter part of my marathon project, I also started looking at my nutritional needs, realizing that I was asking my body to perform at a level that required different sustenance. All of this has been a process of refinement over the years. Again, I can't stress enough how important it is to listen to your body and adjust along the way.

What types of cross-training do you do?

I have dabbled in cycling. I did a century (100-mile road bike race) with my sister. In training for that, I did several smaller bike races. I enjoyed it, but it took so much time, which I didn't enjoy. I have been practicing yoga for about half of my running career. I found it important to stretch out my muscles because running makes them tight. In the winter, I can be found on the slopes enjoying downhill skiing with my family, and I love to waterski in the summer.

I am willing to do pretty much anything to be outside! I recently learned to surf while vacationing in Hawaii, and I love to do stand-up paddleboarding (SUP), hike, and go for walks around the neighborhood in evening. Above all, I think motherhood is the best cross-training exercise there is. Squatting down to pick up and hug my babies strengthens my arms, back, and core. Keeping up with them is a form of speedwork. Bending over to pick up toys doubles as stretching. And all of the joys of motherhood help keep my priorities and ego in check.

What kind of shoes do you run in?

My first running shoes were New Balances. I went to a running store and they did a foot analysis to find out the pressure points of my foot, and that was their recommendation. Once I found a shoe that was comfortable and allowed me to train without injury, I stuck with it. I buy my

shoes in bulk from a discount website. It is easier for me to buy several pair of shoes at once rather than making lots of shopping trips as needed. I find that it is also much cheaper because I can usually find my shoe in last year's model for a reduced price.

I do not track the number of miles on my shoes. I listen to my body and use my joints as an indicator on when to rotate my shoes. If my knees or hips start to hurt, I know it is time for a new pair.

The best advice I received regarding shoes was to buy them a little bigger than I my normal size wear so my toes don't constantly bump into the top of the shoe. In all the marathons I have run, I have only lost one toenail (in the Hatfield McCoy Marathon) and I have only gotten two blisters on my feet.

Do you run year-round outside?

I try to run outside year-round, mostly because I enjoy running with friends but also because I love nature and fresh air. I live where there is a lot of snow and ice in the wintertime, making it important to wear tracks to keep from slipping, as well as warm running clothes. I have down jackets, fleece-lined pants, ski socks, and the best gloves money can buy. I draw the line at zero degrees though. My lungs hurt when it gets that cold!

My husband travels a lot and when my kids were babies, I had to be home in case they needed me. I have a treadmill there that I will use. Since they were little, I wasn't willing to leave them alone while my husband traveled, but

I did have a half-mile loop in my neighborhood around my house that I would often run so I could be outside, yet be close to home.

The only time I was religious about running on the treadmill was when I was pregnant over wintertime. My balance shifted as my stomach got larger and I didn't want to risk falling on the baby. Icy conditions made me nervous and I didn't ever want to take chances the safety of my unborn baby. Plus, I would usually get a lot of stares when I went for a run outside with a big belly!

Have you ever hired a coach?
No, I haven't. However, a guy I worked for early in my professional career was a very talented runner and I learned a lot from him. I have found friends along the way who have had technical training, who ran in college, and who have shared their knowledge with me. I have been able to get this far on my own. I am ready for that next step, though, and will be hiring a coach for my next goal. I did hire a nutritionist who helped me learn how to properly fuel my body. I was very uneducated in this area and I needed help.

What is the hardest part of marathon training?
The hardest part of marathon training is finding balance between my personal needs and the needs of those around me. Marathon training takes dedication. I get up early in the morning and do most of my running before my family wakes up. Aside from my weekends away, they don't see this part of my life. This is one of the main reasons I

wanted to write a book: to share with them what I have learned while they were snuggled up in bed.

I have been told that I am selfish for having such a big goal that is just for myself. While I can understand how some people might think spending so much time on myself (even if the family is asleep) is selfish, I think they reap a lot more benefits by having a healthy, active mother as a model. I don't feel guilty for having this hobby because I know how much I have sacrificed personally to be present in their lives. Not everyone shares that view, but I don't give any weight to those opinions. Still, the words can be hurtful at times.

What is the best part of marathon training?
I have learned more about myself and life through running. I love the perspective it has given me about challenges, failure, persistence, hard work, and setting goals. I love how my children get to see me implement this in my life.

I have also loved what I've experienced with my running friends, whom I've spent many, many hours with over the years. I have seen a young woman lose 45 pounds, I have seen a middle-aged mother gain self-confidence, and I have run with a friend through her divorce. I saw how therapeutic running was for each of them. I find nothing more satisfying than watching and being a part of someone's life as they gain the confidence that will forever change them. It is the best feeling in the world—other than crossing that finish line myself.

Biggest misconception?

I love to run marathons, but the biggest misconception is that it's easy for me. At mile 18 my body starts to hurt and at mile 23 I would love nothing more than a hot shower and a Diet Coke. I find marathons satisfying, but they are still hard.

Have you seen any negative side effects from running this much?

The side effects of running have been largely positive. I have become more confident in myself, in all aspects of my life. I have also used running to process my feelings, instead of turning to other vices. There have been so many wonderful benefits from running, but only a few negative drawbacks. Physically, I am anemic and have amenorrhea, which affect my current and future physical health. I take supplements to offset the damage.

What is next?

As my marathon time has dropped, I am now in the neighborhood of being able to qualify for the Olympic Trials. This thought alone gives me goosebumps! I remember running my first marathon, not knowing if I could even finish. When I realized that I had qualified for Boston, I was so overcome with happiness that the tears started flowing. I felt electric at the very thought of participating in the Boston Marathon. After all these years and all these marathons, I now feel that same excitement and hopefulness when I think about qualifying to participate in the Olympic Trials.

Time will tell if my body is able to withstand the training necessary to achieve that goal. If running a marathon in all 50 states has taught me anything, it is to set my goals high and work hard. I will transfer that same work ethic and dedication to this new goal. A mantra I repeat to myself often is, "If your dreams don't scare you, they aren't big enough." This dream is a little scary to me, but I accept the challenge!